Letts
gets you through

MATHS
TIMED ASSESSMENT PRACTICE TESTS

PRE-TEST
FOR 11+ AND 13+ ENTRY

Ages 10–12

MATHS PRE-TEST

FOR INDEPENDENT SCHOOL ENTRANCE

TIMED ASSESSMENT PRACTICE TESTS

FAISAL NASIM

Contents

About this book 3

Test 1: 10 minutes 4

Test 2: 10 minutes 7

Test 3: 20 minutes 10

Test 4: 20 minutes 15

Test 5: 30 minutes 20

Test 6: 30 minutes 28

Test 7: 50 minutes 36

Test 8: 50 minutes 48

Maths dictionary 61

Answers 67

ACKNOWLEDGEMENTS

Developed by Letts Educational in partnership with Exam Papers Plus (www.exampapersplus.co.uk) to benefit from their combined curriculum knowledge and assessment expertise.

The authors and publisher are grateful to the copyright holders for permission to use quoted materials and images. p

Every effort has been made to trace copyright holders and obtain their permission for the use of copyright material. The author and publisher will gladly receive information enabling them to rectify any error or omission in subsequent editions. All facts are correct at time of going to press.

Published by Letts Educational
An imprint of HarperCollins*Publishers*

1 London Bridge Street
London SE1 9GF

ISBN: 978-1-84419-909-9

First published 2018

10 9 8 7 6 5 4 3 2 1

© HarperCollins*Publishers* Limited 2018

All rights reserved. No part of this publication may be reproduced, stored in a retrieval system, or transmitted, in any form or by any means, electronic, mechanical, photocopying, recording or otherwise, without the prior permission of Letts Educational.

British Library Cataloguing in Publication Data.

A CIP record of this book is available from the British Library.

Commissioning Editors: Michelle I'Anson and Alison James
Author: Faisal Nasim, Exam Papers Plus
Editor and Project Manager: Rebecca Skinner
Cover Design: Sarah Duxbury
Inside Concept Design, Text Design and Layout: Q2A Media
Production: Natalia Rebow
Printed in Great Britain by Martins the Printers

About this book

Pre-tests form part of the 11+ and 13+ admissions process at an increasing number of independent schools across the country. They are usually taken in Year 6 or 7, in an online, multiple-choice format. This book is designed to help students prepare for the maths component of such tests.

Familiarisation with test-style questions is a critical step in preparing your child for any tests they might be required to take as part of a school's admissions process.

This book provides your child with lots of opportunities to test themselves, with practice tests that gradually increase in length, to help build their confidence and improve their chance of success. It contains 8 tests designed to develop key numeracy skills and exam skills.

The level expected can vary greatly from school to school. At the most competitive schools, your child would be expected to be working ahead of national averages and expectations for their age. With this in mind, the tests in this book are designed to be challenging – they include skills and knowledge from the whole Key Stage 2 National Curriculum, including some basic Key Stage 3 skills, which are often introduced towards the end of Key Stage 2.

- Each test is designed to be completed within a short amount of time, with the longest being 50 minutes. Frequent, short bursts of practice are found to be more productive than lengthier sessions.

- Pre-tests and similar assessments can be quite time pressured, so these practice tests will help your child become accustomed to completing questions under such conditions.

- We recommend that your child uses a pencil to complete the tests, so that they can rub out the answers and try again at a later date if necessary.

- Your child should complete the tests in a quiet place where they will not be disturbed. They will need a pencil and rubber to complete the tests, as well as some spare paper for rough working. They will also need to be able to see a clock / watch.

- Your child should **not** use a calculator for any of these tests.

- The first test includes an example question to show your child how to select their answers.

- Answers to all questions are provided at the back of the book, with methods and explanations where appropriate.

- After completing each test, you should go over any incorrect responses with your child to ensure that they understand the reasons for their mistakes and the principles behind each question.

Test 1

You have 10 minutes to complete this test.

You have 10 questions to complete within the given time.

Circle the letter above the correct answer.

EXAMPLE

What is the area of the square?

5 cm

A	B	C	(D)	E
20 cm²	10 cm²	30 cm²	25 cm²	50 cm²

(1) What is this number in figures?

nine thousand, eight hundred and forty-two

A	B	C	D	E
9482	9842	98 822	4298	94 820

(2) What is the missing number in this sequence?

555   563   571   ☐   587

A	B	C	D	E
581	573	579	588	572

③ How many of the small rectangles will it take to fill the square?

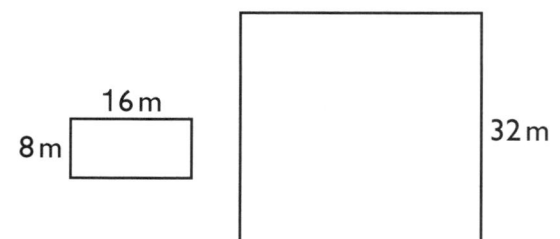

A	B	C	D	E
5	6	4	8	10

④ Garth is 7 cm taller than Ivan.
Ivan is 1·32 m tall.

How tall is Garth in metres?

A	B	C	D	E
1·25 m	1·32 m	2.02 m	1·39 m	1·45 m

⑤ What fraction of this shape is shaded?

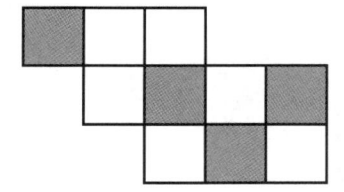

A	B	C	D	E
$\frac{1}{5}$	$\frac{6}{10}$	$\frac{4}{5}$	$\frac{3}{8}$	$\frac{2}{5}$

⑥ $7453 \div X = 7453$

What is the value of X?

A	B	C	D	E
7453	7·453	0	1	10

Questions continue on the next page

⑦ a + 8 = 17 + 15

a = ?

A	B	C	D	E
24	2	32	5	19

⑧ Doris earns £7·50 per week.

How many weeks will it take her to earn £60?

A	B	C	D	E
4 weeks	18 weeks	8 weeks	2 weeks	75 weeks

⑨ All the students at a school are put into groups, labelled A–J.

The number of students in each group is shown in this chart.

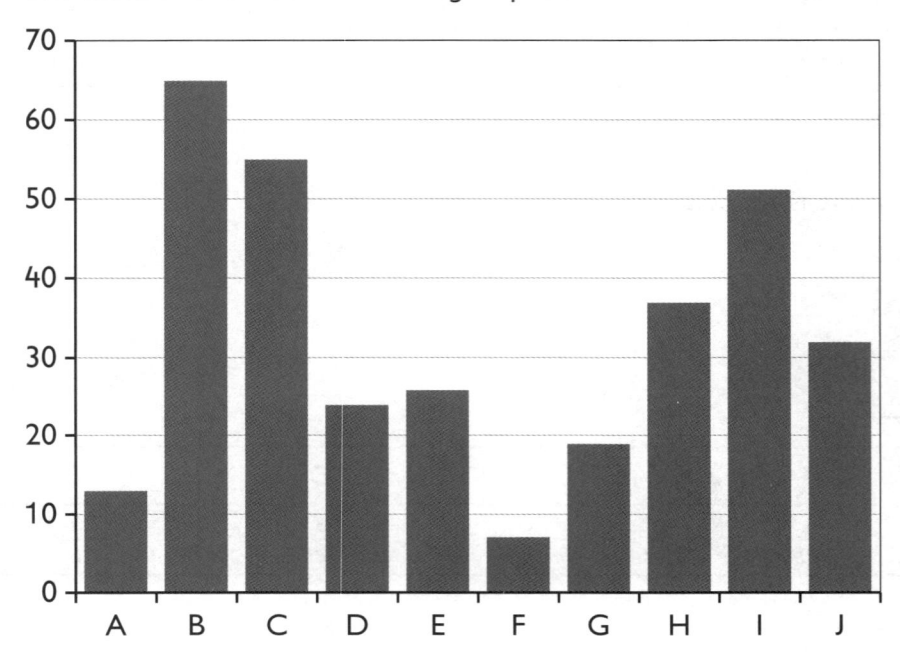

How many groups contain more than 20 students?

A	B	C	D	E
4	5	6	7	8

⑩ The radius of Circle A is double the diameter of Circle B.

How many times greater is the diameter of Circle A than the radius of Circle B?

A	B	C	D	E
2 times greater	4 times greater	6 times greater	8 times greater	10 times greater

Score: .... / 10

Test 2

You have 10 minutes to complete this test.

You have 10 questions to complete within the given time.

Circle the letter above the correct answer.

① The pie chart shows how much time Amanda spends working on different projects every day for one week.
She spends a total of 8 hours per day working on these projects.

How long does Amanda spend working on Project 3 in total?

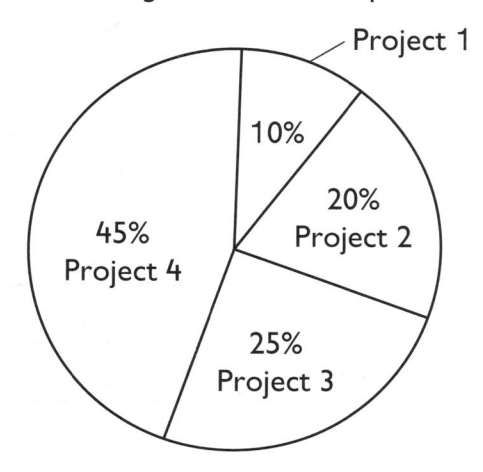

Pie chart:
- Project 1: 10%
- Project 2: 20%
- Project 3: 25%
- Project 4: 45%

A	B	C	D	E
2 hours	8 hours	14 hours	6 hours	25 hours

② A bus left at 3·40 p.m. and returned $2\frac{1}{3}$ hours later.

At what time did the bus return?

A	B	C	D	E
5·50 p.m.	4·20 p.m.	6·20 p.m.	5·10 p.m.	6·00 p.m.

③ A lorry travelled 600 km in 15 hours.

What was the lorry's average speed in kilometres per hour?

A	B	C	D	E
15 kph	20 kph	40 kph	55 kph	60 kph

Questions continue on the next page

④ 35 ÷ ❖ = 21·6 − 4·1

What is the value of ❖?

A	B	C	D	E
7	5	2·8	2	17·5

⑤ Which of these shapes is **not** a pentagon?

A	B	C	D	E

⑥ The cost of manufacturing 20 tiles is £3·50

What is the cost of manufacturing 70 tiles?

A	B	C	D	E
£12·25	£14·00	£2·80	£35·00	£13·50

⑦ Here is part of a train timetable.

Golford	17:31	—	18:41	19:17
Derayston	17:42	18:15	18:59	19:34
Harley	—	18:29	19:18	19:55
Upperton	18:23	—	—	20:17
Baldington	18:56	19:10	19:42	—

Bari is travelling from Derayston.
He needs to arrive at Baldington by 19:00 at the latest.

At what time is the train that Bari should take from Derayston?

A	B	C	D	E
17:31	17:42	18:15	18:23	18:56

8 What is 60 as a percentage of 40?

A	B	C	D	E
66%	40%	120%	150%	20%

9 The standard price for a theatre ticket is £8·20 per person.
In a special offer, orders of 5 tickets or more are charged at 10% less than the standard price.
Renn orders 7 tickets.

How much does Renn save per ticket compared to the standard price?

A	B	C	D	E
£8·20	£5·74	£57·40	£0·82	£32·80

10 Look at this angle.

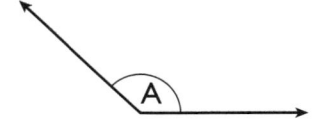

Which of the following best describes Angle A?

A	B	C	D	E
reflex angle	acute angle	right angle	obtuse angle	angle of 230°

Score: ………… / 10

Test 3

You have 20 minutes to complete this test.

You have 20 questions to complete within the given time.

Circle the letter above or alongside the correct answer.

① 8272·6 ÷ 100 =

A	B	C	D	E
82·726	8·2726	827·26	8272·6	82726

② There are 750 apples in a cart.
$\frac{1}{3}$ of the apples are sold and half of the remainder are thrown away.

How many apples are left in the cart?

A	B	C	D	E
750	250	300	500	150

③ A recycling machine processes 671 plastic cups per day.

How many plastic cups does the recycling machine process in August?

A	B	C	D	E
20 130	20 801	20 108	28 011	20 811

④ Which number comes next in this sequence?

15   16   20   29   45   ?

A	B	C	D	E
47	61	70	57	75

5 Last year, a calf weighed 231 kg.
This year, the calf weighs 10% more.

How much does the calf weigh this year?

A	B	C	D	E
254·1 kg	23·1 kg	207·9 kg	231 kg	241 kg

6 The average winter temperature in Blokov is −14°C.
The average spring temperature in Blokov is 9·5°C higher than the average winter temperature.

What is the average spring temperature in Blokov?

A	B	C	D	E
4·5°C	23·5°C	−23·5°C	−18°C	−4·5°C

7 Put these fractions in order of size, starting with the smallest.

$\frac{1}{4}$ $\frac{1}{8}$ $\frac{3}{4}$ $\frac{5}{8}$ $\frac{3}{9}$ $\frac{8}{10}$

A	$\frac{1}{8}$	$\frac{1}{4}$	$\frac{5}{8}$	$\frac{3}{9}$	$\frac{3}{4}$	$\frac{8}{10}$
B	$\frac{1}{4}$	$\frac{1}{8}$	$\frac{3}{9}$	$\frac{5}{8}$	$\frac{3}{4}$	$\frac{8}{10}$
C	$\frac{1}{8}$	$\frac{1}{4}$	$\frac{3}{9}$	$\frac{5}{8}$	$\frac{3}{4}$	$\frac{8}{10}$
D	$\frac{1}{8}$	$\frac{1}{4}$	$\frac{3}{9}$	$\frac{3}{4}$	$\frac{5}{8}$	$\frac{8}{10}$
E	$\frac{1}{8}$	$\frac{1}{4}$	$\frac{5}{8}$	$\frac{3}{4}$	$\frac{3}{9}$	$\frac{8}{10}$

Questions continue on the next page

8 Look at this diagram.

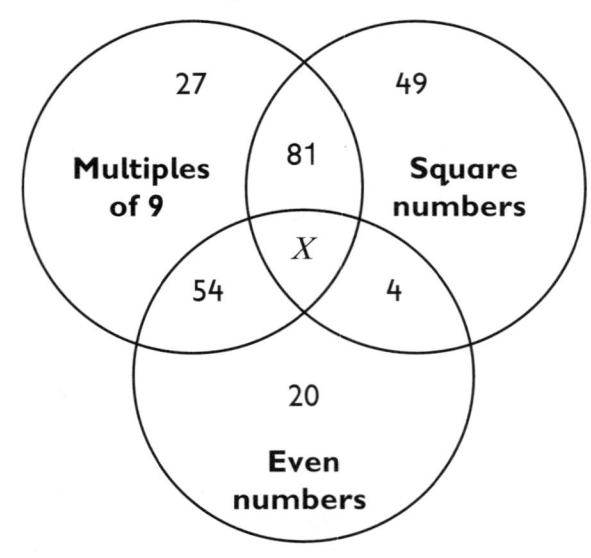

[Venn diagram with three circles labeled "Multiples of 9", "Square numbers", and "Even numbers". Values: 27 (Multiples of 9 only), 49 (Square numbers only), 81 (Multiples of 9 ∩ Square numbers), 54 (Multiples of 9 ∩ Even numbers), 4 (Square numbers ∩ Even numbers), 20 (Even numbers only), X (intersection of all three).]

Which of the following could be the value of X?

A	B	C	D	E
18	36	25	64	63

9 7·622 + 13·329 =

A	B	C	D	E
20·951	20·519	20·591	20·195	20·159

10 Which arrow is pointing to 4·7?

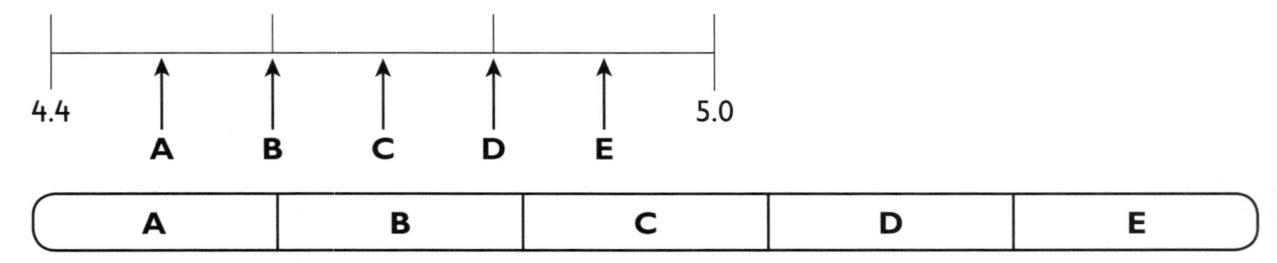

[Number line from 4.4 to 5.0 with arrows A, B, C, D, E]

A	B	C	D	E

11 The coordinates of Point B are (5, −8).
Point C is a reflection of Point B in the x-axis.

What are the coordinates of Point C?

A	B	C	D	E
(5, −8)	(−5, −8)	(5, 8)	(−8, 5)	(8, −5)

12 Which number should go in the box?

756 × 321 = 242 676

75·6 × 321 = ☐

A	B	C	D	E
242 676	242·676	2426·76	24 267·6	24·2676

13 A bus can transport 52 passengers.

How many buses are needed to transport 421 passengers?

A	B	C	D	E
7	8	9	10	11

14 $48 \times 7 + 4 = 223 + X$

What is the value of X?

A	B	C	D	E
48	305	248	117	171

15 Cube A has a volume of 64 cm³.

What is the area of one face of Cube A?

A	B	C	D	E
64 cm²	36 cm²	6 cm²	4 cm²	16 cm²

16 How many more edges than faces does this shape have?

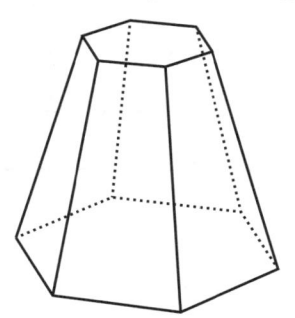

A	B	C	D	E
8	24	18	10	6

Questions continue on the next page

17 This is a diagram of Cuboid A.

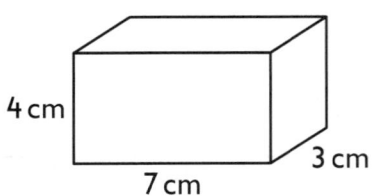

4 cm, 7 cm, 3 cm

The length of Cuboid B is twice the length of Cuboid A.
The width of Cuboid B is twice the width of Cuboid A.
The height of Cuboid B is three times the height of Cuboid A.

What is the volume of Cuboid B?

A	B	C	D	E
84 cm³	252 cm³	672 cm³	1008 cm³	504 cm³

18 How many times greater is 247 than 13?

A	B	C	D	E
260	14	17	19	234

19 The ratio of peaches, apples and bananas in a box is 7:5:3

If there are 100 apples in the box, how many more peaches are there than bananas?

A	B	C	D	E
70	80	4	140	60

20 The mean weight of 5 turnips in a bag was 4·5 kg.
One more turnip was added to the bag and the mean weight of the turnips became 4·6 kg.

What was the weight of the turnip that was added to the bag?

A	B	C	D	E
4·5 kg	5·1 kg	4·6 kg	5·5 kg	5·3 kg

Score: .... / 20

Test 4

You have 20 minutes to complete this test.
You have 20 questions to complete within the given time.

Circle the letter above the correct answer.

1) If I change £3·60 into 20p coins, how many coins will I get?

A	B	C	D	E
20 coins	30 coins	15 coins	18 coins	36 coins

2) This chart shows the population of Skeggerith in different years.

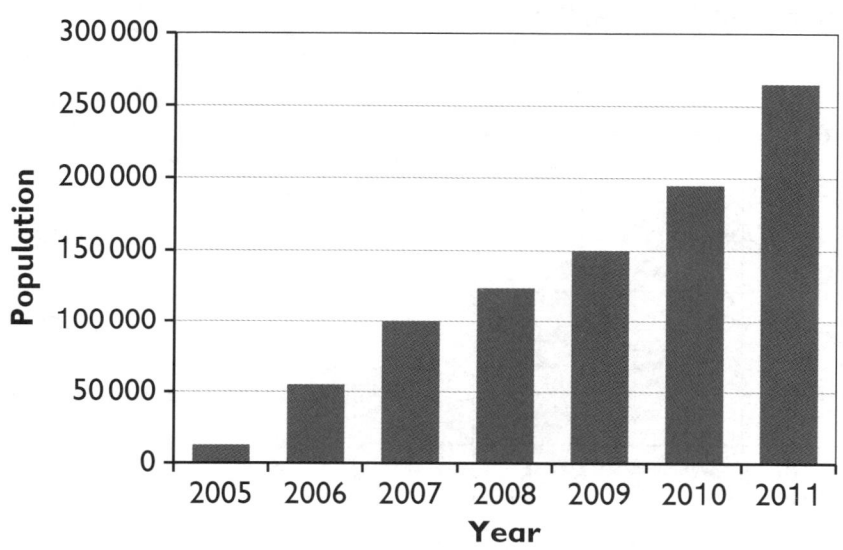

Between which two years was there the greatest percentage increase in population?

A	B	C	D	E
2005 and 2006	2006 and 2007	2008 and 2009	2009 and 2010	2010 and 2011

3) The perimeter of a regular hexagon is 40·2 cm.

What is the total length of 2 sides of the hexagon?

A	B	C	D	E
80·4 cm	13·4 cm	20·1 cm	25 cm	6·7 cm

Questions continue on the next page

④ Change the order of the figures 89 283 to make the second smallest number possible.

A	B	C	D	E
23 889	23 998	32 898	23 898	28 938

⑤ The time in Hong Kong is 8 hours ahead of the time in London.
It takes $11\frac{1}{2}$ hours to fly from London to Hong Kong.
A plane takes off from London at 2·30 p.m. local time.

What will the local time in Hong Kong be when the plane lands there?

A	B	C	D	E
02:00	11:30	14:30	22:00	10:00

⑥ This grid shows the coordinates of Points A, B and D.

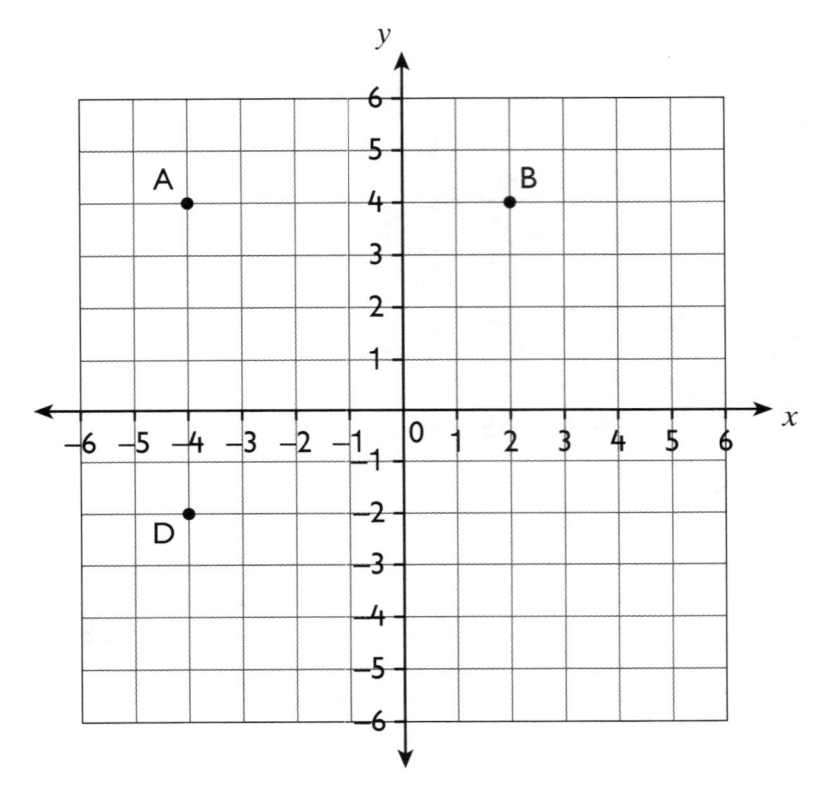

The points A, B, C and D join together to form a square.

What are the coordinates of Point C?

A	B	C	D	E
(−4, −3)	(2, 2)	(−2, 2)	(2, −2)	(3, −2)

16

7 Write this number in figures:

four hundred thousand and nineteen

A	B	C	D	E
400 019	419 000	400 109	400 190	401 900

8 How many eighths are there in $7\frac{3}{4}$?

A	B	C	D	E
56 eighths	59 eighths	63 eighths	24 eighths	62 eighths

9 Divide 3600 into 18 equal parts.

What is the value of each part?

A	B	C	D	E
100	36	20	180	200

10 What fraction of this square is shaded?

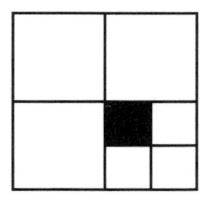

A	B	C	D	E
$\frac{1}{4}$	$\frac{1}{3}$	$\frac{1}{20}$	$\frac{1}{16}$	$\frac{1}{12}$

11 What is the value of the 8 in the number 456·783

A	B	C	D	E
8 tens	8 thousandths	8 hundreds	8 tenths	8 hundredths

Questions continue on the next page

(12) 6 boys eat 6 doughnuts each and 4 girls eat 4 doughnuts each.

What is the mean number of doughnuts eaten per child?
Round your answer to the nearest whole number.

A	B	C	D	E
3 doughnuts	4 doughnuts	5 doughnuts	6 doughnuts	7 doughnuts

(13) $\frac{15}{45} = \frac{20}{\triangle}$

What is the value of $\triangle$?

A	B	C	D	E
3	45	50	60	80

(14) Trevor has £110

He spends half of this amount on a new video game.

He also buys 2 books for £7·50 each and a magazine for £4·50

How much money does Trevor have left?

A	B	C	D	E
£85	£35·50	£74·50	£43	£40·50

(15) This chart shows the number of buses manufactured in a factory each month.

Aug: 9 buses
July: 8 buses
June: 7 buses
May: 6 buses
Apr: 6 buses
Mar: 5 buses
Feb: 4 buses
Jan: 3 buses

← Number of buses manufactured →

🚌 = 10 buses

How many buses were manufactured in total in April, July and August?

A	B	C	D	E
22	240	26	24	180

16 Mary has a piece of ribbon that measures 1·5 m.

She cuts it in half and then cuts each of the halves into 7 equal pieces.

How many pieces of ribbon does Mary now have?

A	B	C	D	E
7	2	14	140	15

17 Two angles in a triangle are 75° and 18°.

What is the size of the third angle in the triangle?

A	B	C	D	E
15°	93°	84°	87°	90°

18 What is the missing number in this sequence?

45 35 ? 18 11 5

A	B	C	D	E
26	25	33	45	29

19 (48 − 7) × 3 =

A	B	C	D	E
27	123	108	21	121

20 Beni fills this jug with water up to the point marked by the arrow.

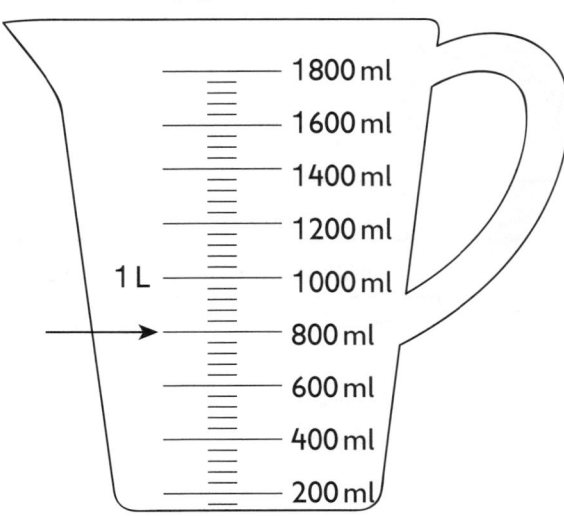

How much water is there in the jug?

A	B	C	D	E
8 litres	0.008 litres	0·8 litres	0.08 litres	800 litres

Score: .... / 20

Test 5

You have 30 minutes to complete this test.

You have 30 questions to complete within the given time.

Circle the letter above or alongside the correct answer.

1) 486 ÷ 9 =

A	B	C	D	E
51	52	53	54	55

2) Look at these containers.

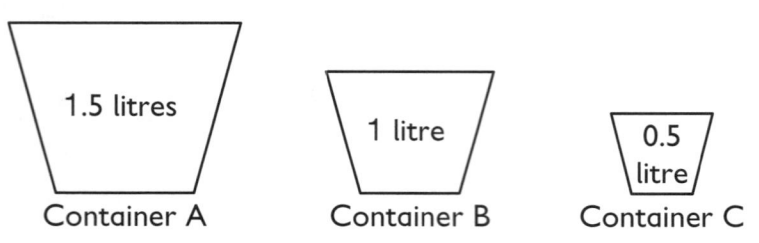

Container A — 1.5 litres
Container B — 1 litre
Container C — 0.5 litre

How many times greater is the capacity of Container A than the capacity of Container C?

A	B	C	D	E
1	2	3	4	5

3) Robert has a collection of 336 stamps.

$\frac{1}{3}$ of these stamps are blue.

How many of Robert's stamps are **not** blue?

A	B	C	D	E
112 stamps	88 stamps	336 stamps	168 stamps	224 stamps

4) The cost of a chair is £25·50

Fiona wants to buy 4 chairs.

She currently has £18·00

How much more money does Fiona need to buy the chairs?

A	B	C	D	E
£102·00	£25·50	£7·50	£84·00	£120·00

5) Which of these numbers is closest to 0·6?

A	B	C	D	E
0·65	0·58	0·585	0·601	0·61001

6) Put these numbers in order, from largest to smallest.

0·175   0·715   0·158   0·164

A	0·715 0·175 0·164 0·158
B	0·158 0·715 0·164 0·175
C	0·158 0·164 0·175 0·715
D	0·715 0·164 0·158 0·175
E	0·715 0·175 0·158 0·164

7) 3 lemons cost £1·56

What is the cost of 7 lemons?

A	B	C	D	E
£0·52	£3·12	£3·64	£3·02	£3·44

8) What is 120% of 35?

A	B	C	D	E
36	7	45	70	42

9) The length of this rectangle is twice its width.

7.5 cm

What is the perimeter of the rectangle?

A	B	C	D	E
7·5 cm	15 cm	30 cm	37·5 cm	45 cm

Questions continue on the next page

10 This bar chart shows how many people of different nationalities visited a certain theme park in one year.

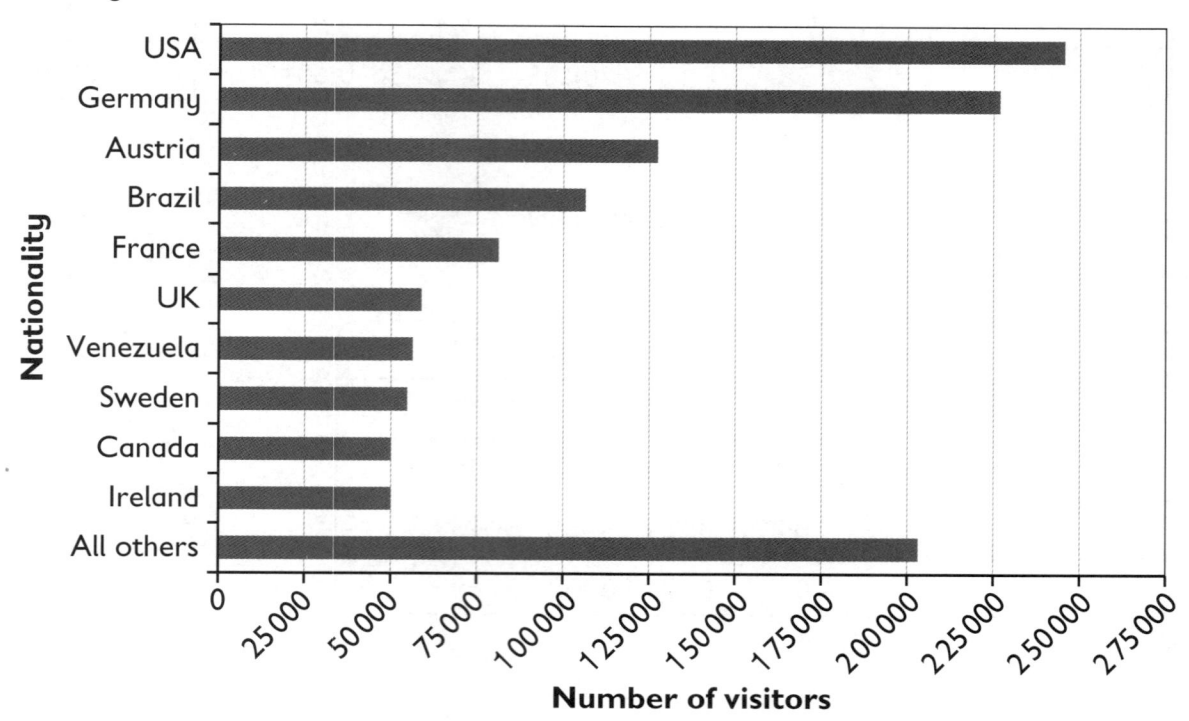

Which of the following statements is **false**?

A	There were more visitors from France than from the UK.
B	The largest number of visitors came from the USA.
C	There were more visitors from Venezuela than from Ireland.
D	There were fewer visitors from Brazil than from Sweden.
E	Visitors from Austria outnumbered those from Canada.

11 Eva spent $1\frac{3}{4}$ hours reading.

She finished reading at 2·21 p.m.

At what time did Eva begin reading?

A	B	C	D	E
12·30 p.m.	1·21 p.m.	4·06 p.m.	12·36 p.m.	12·45 p.m.

12 $\frac{4}{5}$ of A has the same value as $\frac{2}{3}$ of B.

If $B = 60$, what is the value of A?

A	B	C	D	E
48	40	55	50	20

(13) Which of the moves described in the table is **not** a rotation?

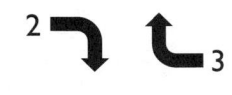

A	B	C	D	E
5 → 2	1 → 5	3 → 5	4 → 2	1 → 3

(14) The diameter of a circle is 15·5 cm.

What is the radius of the circle?

A	B	C	D	E
31 cm	7·5 cm	7 cm	32 cm	7·75 cm

(15) Winny's monthly rent is £550

She also spends £225 per month on gas and electricity.

How much does Winny spend per year on rent, gas and electricity?

A	B	C	D	E
£6600	£9300	£775	£2700	£11 000

(16) This diagram shows a scalene triangle and a straight line.

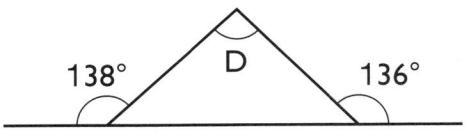

What is the size of angle D?

A	B	C	D	E
94°	44°	86°	55°	42°

Questions continue on the next page

(17) This diagram shows the distance in kilometres driven by Fred along a track.

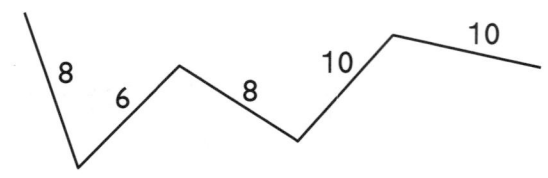

8, 6, 8, 10, 10

It took Fred 45 minutes to drive the full distance.

What was Fred's average speed in kilometres per hour?

A	B	C	D	E
56 kph	42 kph	60 kph	45 kph	25 kph

(18) A skip full of rubbish weighs 420 kg.

When empty, the skip weighs 102·5 kg.

What is the weight of the rubbish?

A	B	C	D	E
315 kg	322·5 kg	317·5 kg	522·5 kg	319 kg

(19) The table shows the total number of grapes picked by different workers over 5 days.

Worker's name	Number of grapes
Bob	1348
Dev	2311
Diana	3213
Cali	2568

What was the mean number of grapes picked per worker per day?

A	B	C	D	E
2360 grapes	1888 grapes	9440 grapes	3482 grapes	472 grapes

20) The shape below is formed from identical squares, each with a side length of 5 cm.

What is the perimeter of the shape?

A	B	C	D	E
100 cm	80 cm	125 cm	65 cm	75 cm

21) $2s + 4b = 81$

If $s = 0.5$, what is the value of b?

A	B	C	D	E
0.5	20	21	20.5	1

22) A cuboid has a width of 5 cm, a height of 10 cm and a volume of 250 cm³.

What is the length of the cuboid?

A	B	C	D	E
50 cm	5 cm	10 cm	25 cm	250 cm

23) I think of a number, divide it by 2, add 8 and then subtract 17

My answer is 10.5

What number did I think of?

A	B	C	D	E
27.5	9.75	18	19.5	39

24) The height of a triangle is three times its base.

If the base of the triangle is 5 cm, what is the area of the triangle?

A	B	C	D	E
75 cm²	37.5 cm²	5 cm²	25 cm²	15 cm²

Questions continue on the next page

25) Imran buys 2 watermelons for £4·65 each and an orange for 55 pence.
He pays with a £10 note.

How much change does Imran receive?

A	B	C	D	E
£0·15	£4·80	£5·20	£9·20	£9·85

26) 0·0282 + 2·7301 = ☐

A	B	C	D	E
2·7538	2·7385	2·7358	2·7583	2·3758

27) What is the size of Angle H?

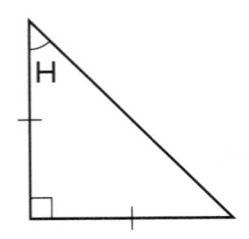

A	B	C	D	E
180°	67·5°	45°	90°	135°

28) This graph shows the conversion rate between pounds (£) and euros (€).

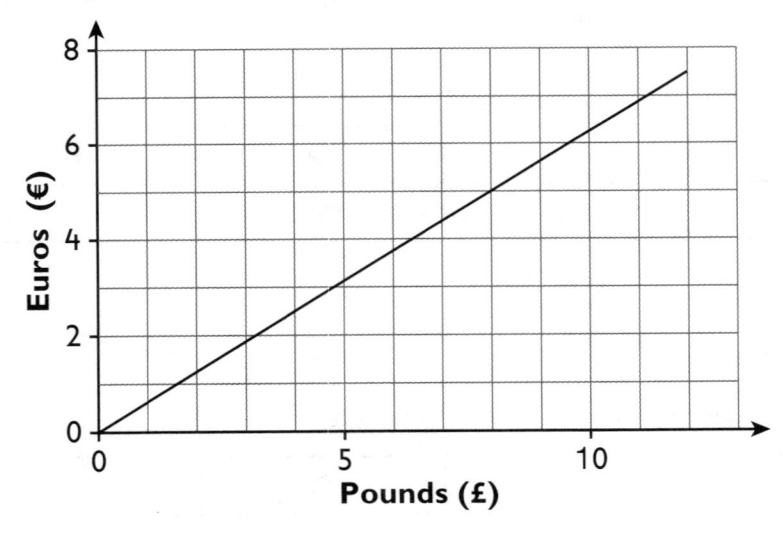

How many euros (€) is £16?

A	B	C	D	E
€16	€5	€8	€10	€22

29 Timothy begins work at 8·47 a.m. and ends work at 4·17 p.m.

For how long does Timothy work?

A	B	C	D	E
$7\frac{1}{2}$ hours	$6\frac{1}{2}$ hours	$7\frac{2}{3}$ hours	$8\frac{1}{4}$ hours	$6\frac{3}{4}$ hours

30 The test scores of the students in Class A are shown below:

87 34 54 34 98 54 34 87 14 37 66 22

What is the difference between the highest score and the lowest score?

A	B	C	D	E
73	84	64	76	58

Score: .... / 30

Test 6

You have 30 minutes to complete this test.

You have 30 questions to complete within the given time.

Circle the letter above the correct answer.

1) What is 45·6508 rounded to 3 decimal places?

A	B	C	D	E
45·650	45·658	45·659	45·651	45·652

2) Fawad buys 3 chocolate bars for y pence each.

He pays with a £10 note.

Which expression shows how much change he receives?

A	B	C	D	E
$-y$	$-3y$	$100 - 3y$	$1000 - 3y$	$1000 - y$

3) The endpoints of five lines are shown in table below.

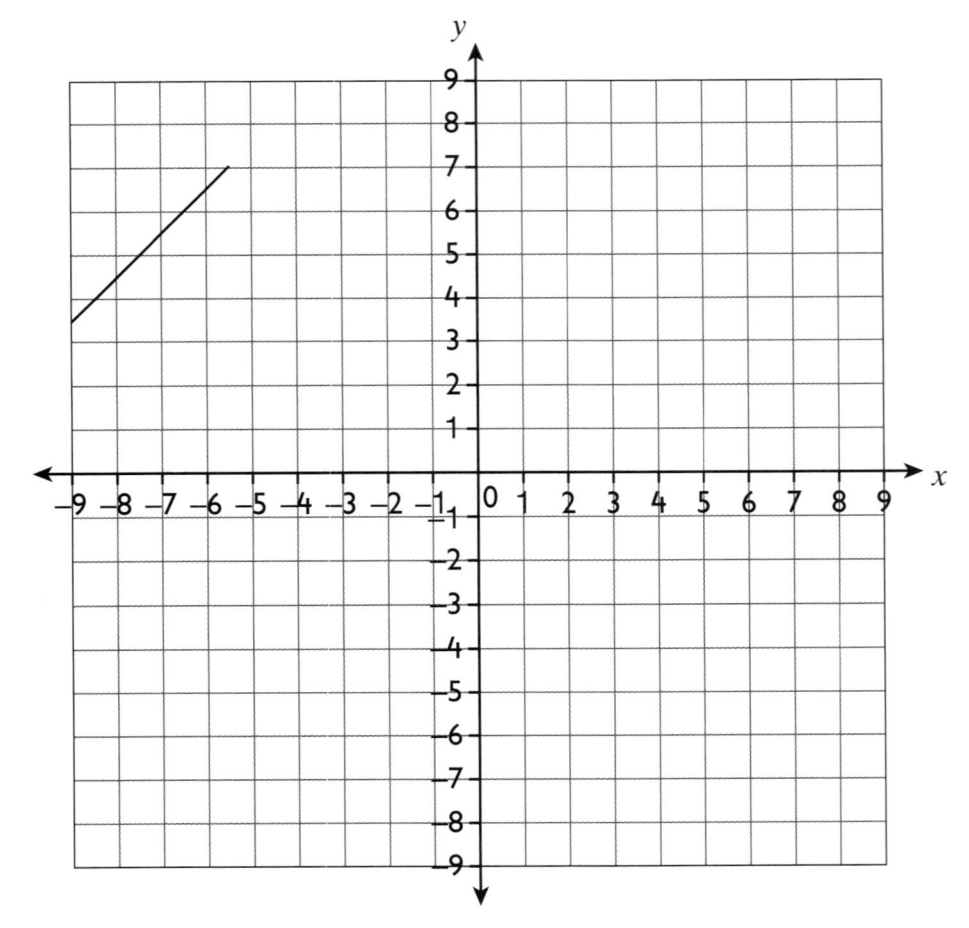

Which line is perpendicular to the line in the diagram?

A	B	C	D	E
(4, 9) and (3, 8)	(−6, 1) and (−1, 6)	(7, 3) and (7, 1)	(0, 0) and (5, −5)	(4, 8) and (−7, 6)

4 What is 1·65 as a fraction?

A	B	C	D	E
$\frac{165}{165}$	$\frac{32}{2}$	$\frac{7}{5}$	$\frac{33}{20}$	$\frac{13}{8}$

5 The width of this rectangle is 3 times smaller than its length.

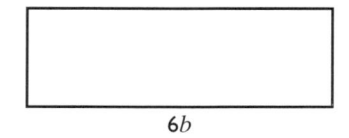

6b

Which expression shows the perimeter of the rectangle?

A	B	C	D	E
$3b$	$16b$	$14b$	$18b$	$24b$

6 This is a Venn diagram.

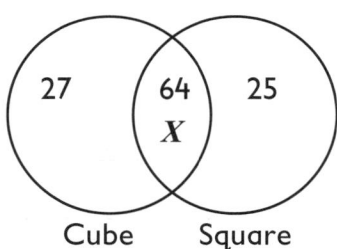

27 | 64 X | 25

Cube numbers | Square numbers

Which of the following could be the value of X?

A	B	C	D	E
36	1	81	9	8

7 The price of a hat is reduced by 15% in a sale.
The reduced price is £85

What was the price of the hat before it was reduced?

A	B	C	D	E
£85	£97	£70	£100	£110

Questions continue on the next page

8 8 pears cost the same as 4 oranges.
2 oranges cost the same as 3 lemons.

If the cost of a lemon is 32 pence, what is the cost of 4 pears?

A	B	C	D	E
64 pence	32 pence	100 pence	96 pence	24 pence

9 Ben plans to cover his bathroom floor with square marble tiles.
The diagrams below show the dimensions of the bathroom floor and 1 square marble tile.

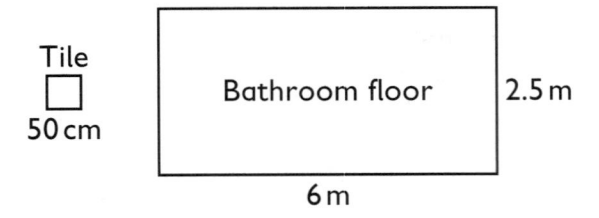

Tile 50 cm

Bathroom floor 2.5 m

6 m

How many marble tiles does Ben need to cover the whole area of the bathroom floor?

A	B	C	D	E
50 tiles	60 tiles	30 tiles	15 tiles	80 tiles

10 If $y = 4$, what is the mean of these expressions?

$3y + 5$ $4y + 6$ $4y - 1$

A	B	C	D	E
3	18	20	54	48

11 A path is laid around the outside of a garden.
The length of the garden is 25 m and its width is 10 m.
The path is 1 m wide.

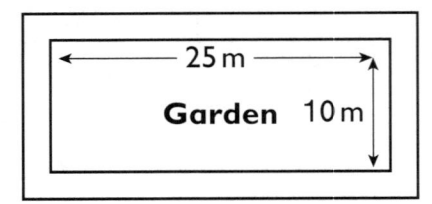

25 m
Garden 10 m

What is the total area of the path and the garden?

A	B	C	D	E
324 m²	250 m²	286 m²	270 m²	348 m²

(12) Look at this table.

Shape	No. of sides	Sum of all angles
Triangle	3	180°
Square	4	

Which of the following should go in the empty cell?

A	B	C	D	E
540°	90°	180°	270°	360°

(13) Rita owns some shares in a company.

The share price rises by 10% and the total value of Rita's shares increases by £10 000

If the price of 1 share before the increase was £50, how many shares does Rita own?

A	B	C	D	E
1000	50	10 000	2000	50 000

(14) For every 7 bananas in a crate, there are 4 oranges.

If there are 132 oranges, how many bananas are there in the crate?

A	B	C	D	E
33 bananas	85 bananas	363 bananas	924 bananas	231 bananas

(15) Tia shares £4·80 equally between herself and two friends.

How much does each friend receive?

A	B	C	D	E
£1·00	£2·40	£1·60	£3·60	£0·80

(16) The volume of a cube is 125 cm³.

What is the surface area of the cube?

A	B	C	D	E
125 cm²	25 cm²	150 cm²	225 cm²	5 cm²

Questions continue on the next page

(17) Neil is facing north-west.

He turns 270° anticlockwise.

Which direction is Neil now facing?

A	B	C	D	E
south-east	east	north-east	south-west	west

(18) The shape below is formed from identical regular pentagons.

Each pentagon has a side length of 7·5 cm.

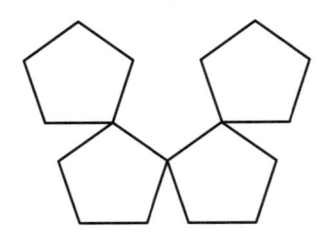

What is the perimeter of the shape?

A	B	C	D	E
7·5 cm	37·5 cm	187·5 cm	75 cm	150 cm

(19) 1·7 × 0·04 =

A	B	C	D	E
0·068	6·8	68·6	0·68	0·0068

(20) Which of the following numbers is a multiple of 9 and 5 but not of 4?

A	B	C	D	E
180	260	200	315	250

(21) Which number should go in the box to complete the sum?

33 × 110 = 3200 + ☐

A	B	C	D	E
280	430	540	330	200

22) Lisa asked 100 students to choose their favourite colour.
She recorded her results in the pie chart below.

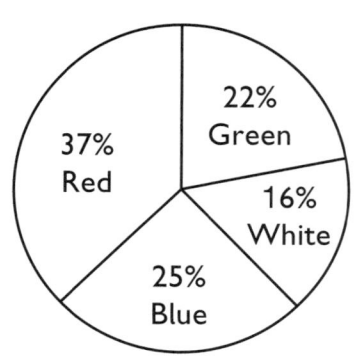

- 37% Red
- 22% Green
- 16% White
- 25% Blue

25% of students chose blue as their favourite colour.

What is the size of the angle in the blue segment of the pie chart?

A	B	C	D	E
34°	45°	25°	90°	135°

23) The three angles in a triangle are $X°$, $5X°$ and $4X°$.

What is the value of $2X°$?

A	B	C	D	E
20°	90°	180°	36°	18°

24) There are 13 children standing in a queue.
There are twice as many children standing in front of Maria than behind her.

In what position in the queue is Maria standing?

A	B	C	D	E
7th	3rd	5th	8th	9th

Questions continue on the next page

(25) The bag below contains black, white and striped balls.

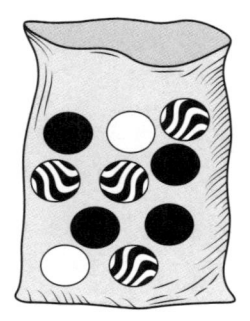

Jaks removes 1 ball at random.

What is the probability that this ball is striped?

A	B	C	D	E
$\frac{2}{10}$	$\frac{4}{5}$	$\frac{3}{8}$	$\frac{1}{5}$	$\frac{2}{5}$

(26) This thermometer shows the temperature in Greenland on Thursday.

The temperature on Friday was 3 degrees greater than on the previous day.

The temperature on Saturday was 7 degrees less than on the previous day.

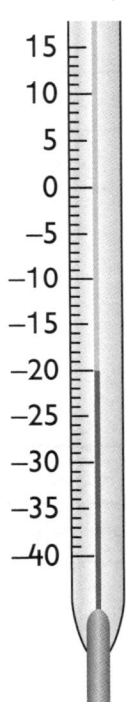

What was the temperature in Greenland on Saturday?

A	B	C	D	E
−24°	−16°	−25°	−17°	−12°

(27) A cup can hold 450 ml of water when full.

A jug can hold 3·5 litres of water when full

Ewan uses a full jug of water to fill $4\frac{1}{2}$ empty cups.

How much water is left in the jug?

A	B	C	D	E
2·025 litres	1·5 litres	0·8 litres	1·7 litres	1·475 litres

(28) On a number line, which number would be halfway between −15 and 25?

A	B	C	D	E
0	5	10	15	20

(29) When the grid below is filled, the numbers in each row and column add up to 33

	10	8
5	?	11
		14

Which number should replace the question mark?

A	B	C	D	E
13	18	17	14	5

(30) What fraction of 7 weeks is a fortnight?

A	B	C	D	E
$\frac{1}{14}$	$\frac{7}{49}$	$\frac{2}{7}$	$\frac{14}{7}$	$\frac{49}{14}$

Score: .... / 30

Test 7

You have 50 minutes to complete this test.

You have 50 questions to complete within the given time.

Circle the letter above or alongside the correct answer.

1) How many eighths are there in 12?

A	B	C	D	E
12	8	18	96	108

2) Which of the following equals 2450?

A	2450 rounded to the nearest 100
B	2366 rounded to the nearest 50
C	2458 rounded to the nearest 10
D	2445 rounded to the nearest 10
E	2480 rounded to the nearest 10

3) This bar chart shows the number of apples eaten by four people over four months.

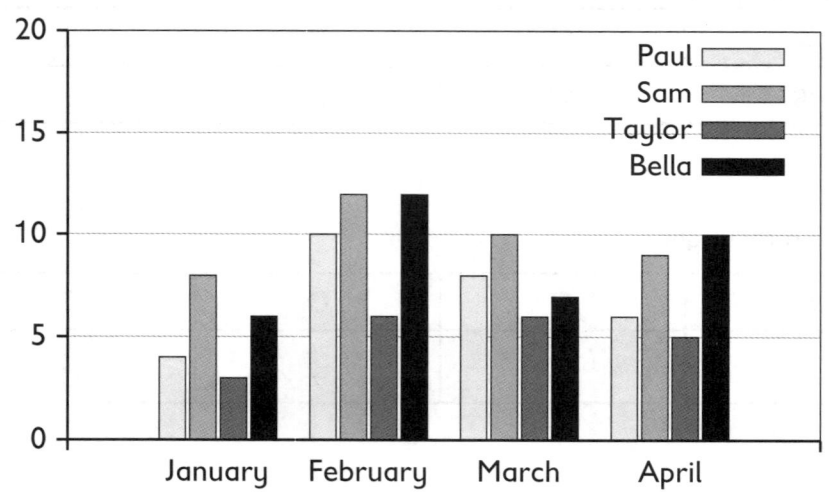

Who ate the most apples in March?

A	B	C	D	E
Paul	Sam	Taylor	Bella	Simon

④ Change the order of the figures 37 281 to make the largest number possible.

A	B	C	D	E
37 281	87 321	87 231	28 123	87 331

⑤ The time in Mumbai is $5\frac{1}{2}$ hours ahead of the time in London.
If it is 02:45 in Mumbai, what is the time in London?

A	B	C	D	E
07:45	08:15	09:15	21:15	21:45

⑥ Which of the following is the best estimate of the size of Angle A?

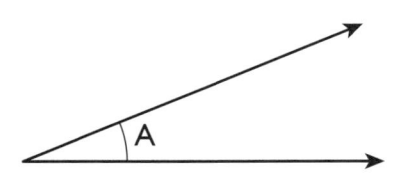

A	B	C	D	E
20°	90°	75°	130°	225°

⑦ 49 + (18 ÷ 6) = ☐

A	B	C	D	E
$11\frac{4}{25}$	54	46	17	52

⑧ How many empty bottles with a capacity of 300 ml can be filled from a jug that contains 4·8 litres of water?

A	B	C	D	E
15 bottles	3 bottles	18 bottles	16 bottles	5 bottles

⑨ What is 37·5% of 80?

A	B	C	D	E
40	37·5	24	32	30

Questions continue on the next page

10 Which of the moves described in the table below is a translation?

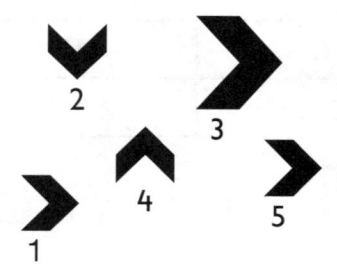

A	B	C	D	E
2 → 3	4 → 5	4 → 3	1 → 3	5 → 1

11 This diagram shows the distance in metres between shops in a city.

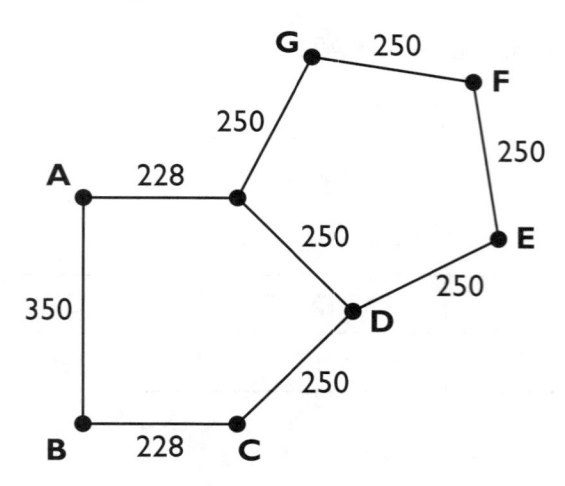

Vijay walks from Shop G to Shop C using the shortest route possible.

How far did Vijay walk?

A	B	C	D	E
0·7 km	1·056 km	0·25 km	1 km	0·75 km

12 I think of a number, subtract it from 75 and then double the result.

My answer is 120

What number did I think of?

A	B	C	D	E
15	135	45	60	30

13 The mean weight of 3 boxes is 3·45 kg.

If 2 of the boxes each weigh 3·5 kg, what is the weight of the third box?

A	B	C	D	E
3·45 kg	3·5 kg	3·35 kg	3·2 kg	3·55 kg

14 Three identical equilateral triangles are drawn.

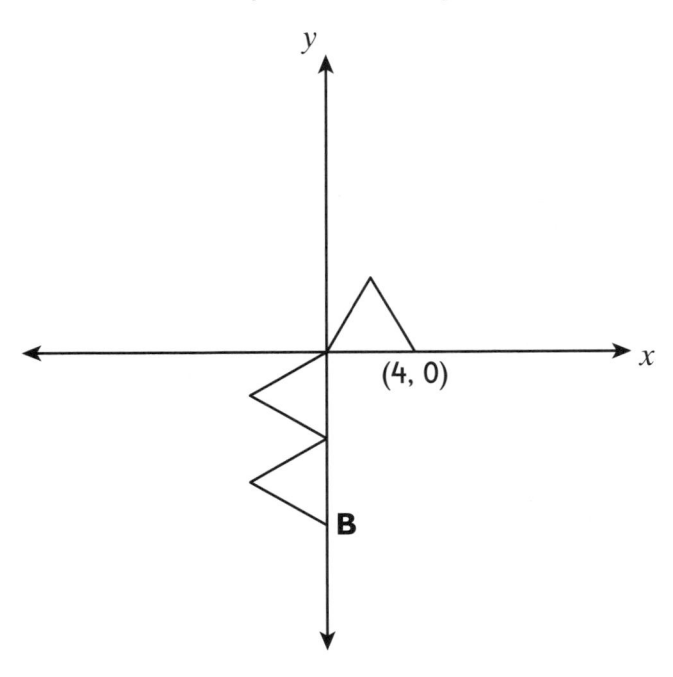

What is the x-coordinate of Point B?

A	B	C	D	E
0	4	8	12	5

15 Tanish faces south-west.

He turns 45° in a clockwise direction.

In which direction is Tanish now facing?

A	B	C	D	E
west	north	south	east	south-east

16 4 tigers take 7 hours to eat 40 kilograms of meat.

How long would it take 8 tigers to eat 80 kilograms of meat?

A	B	C	D	E
6 hours	3·5 hours	14 hours	7 hours	21 hours

Questions continue on the next page

17 The area of a rectangle is 128 cm².
The length of the rectangle is twice its width.

What is the width of the rectangle?

A	B	C	D	E
16 cm	4 cm	8 cm	22 cm	28 cm

18 0·034 + 45·9 = ☐

A	B	C	D	E
49·3	45·934	46·24	45·124	46·233

19 Jake sees the following offer for oranges in the supermarket.

> Buy 3 and get the 4th half price!

An orange costs 44 pence.
Jake buys 15 oranges.

How much does he pay in total?

A	B	C	D	E
£6·60	£6·30	£6·16	£5·94	£5·84

20 What is the sum of the three largest 2-digit whole numbers?

A	B	C	D	E
300	297	294	295	291

21 Garv spent £37·50 buying bags of potatoes.
Each bag cost £2·50 and weighed 750 g.

What was the total weight of the bags of potatoes that Garv bought?

A	B	C	D	E
15 kg	11·25 kg	37·5 kg	2·5 kg	18·75 kg

(22) What is 2·3 expressed as an improper fraction?

A	B	C	D	E
$\frac{2}{3}$	$\frac{23}{3}$	$\frac{46}{20}$	$\frac{45}{2}$	$\frac{5}{3}$

(23) How many squares are there in the diagram below?

A	B	C	D	E
5 squares	6 squares	7 squares	8 squares	9 squares

(24) Which of the following numbers is not prime?

A	B	C	D	E
2	17	1	47	59

(25) The students at Braston School were asked to choose their favourite logo design from four options.

Their choices are shown in the pie chart below.

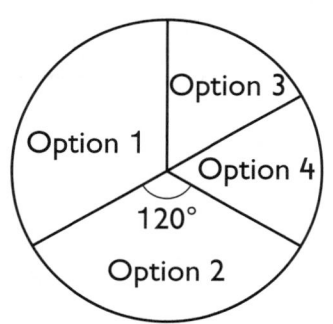

Options 3 and 4 were equally popular.

Options 1 and 2 were equally popular.

If 80 students chose Option 1, how many students were asked in total?

A	B	C	D	E
240	80	160	40	320

Questions continue on the next page

(26) Which number could be the value of Y in this Venn diagram?

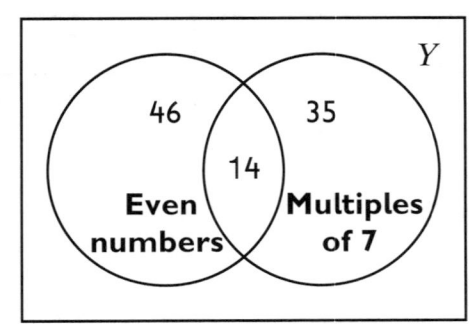

Venn diagram: Even numbers circle contains 46; Multiples of 7 circle contains 35; intersection contains 14; Y is outside both circles.

A	B	C	D	E
44	59	63	56	7

(27) How many months in a year have more than 30 days?

A	B	C	D	E
5	6	7	8	9

(28) $7X + 2Y - 12$
$3X + 8Y + 32$

If $X = 7$ and Y equals the largest 2-digit even number, what is the difference in value between these two expressions?

A	B	C	D	E
233	135	604	568	837

(29) The sum of the angles in Triangle A is 180°.

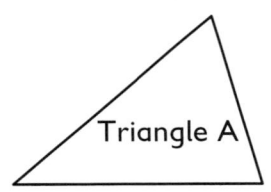

Triangle B is formed by doubling all the sides of Triangle A.

What is the sum of the angles in Triangle B?

A	B	C	D	E
90°	135°	180°	360°	540°

30) The shape below is formed from identical isosceles triangles.

Each triangle has a base of 7 cm and a height of 10 cm.

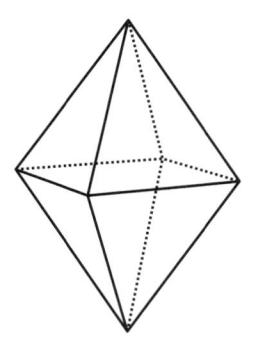

What is the surface area of the shape?

A	B	C	D	E
35 cm²	280 cm²	560 cm²	140 cm²	70 cm²

31) Greg drove 65 kilometres in 75 minutes.

What is Greg's speed in kilometres per hour?

A	B	C	D	E
65 kph	52 kph	45 kph	30 kph	55 kph

32) Each circle below has a diameter of 39 cm.

The centre of each circle is marked by a black dot.

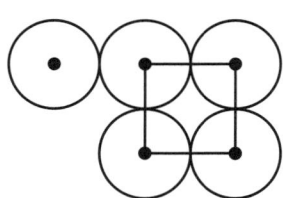

What is the perimeter of the square?

A	B	C	D	E
3·12 m	0·78 m	0·39 m	1·56 m	4·5 m

33) What percentage of £30 is 30 pence?

A	B	C	D	E
30%	3%	10%	300%	1%

Questions continue on the next page

34 Reena draws a shape with exactly 1 pair of parallel lines.
The sum of the angles in Reena's shape is 360°.

What shape did Reena draw?

A	B	C	D	E
square	parallelogram	trapezium	rectangle	kite

35 Which of these is the smallest?

A	B	C	D	E
$\frac{2}{5}$ of 75	half of 62	$\frac{1}{8}$ of 248	30% of 90	9 × 4

36 Which number should go in the box?

67·5 ÷ ☐ = 675

A	B	C	D	E
100	10	1	0·1	0·01

37 This chart shows the rainfall in millimetres in a town during different months in a year.

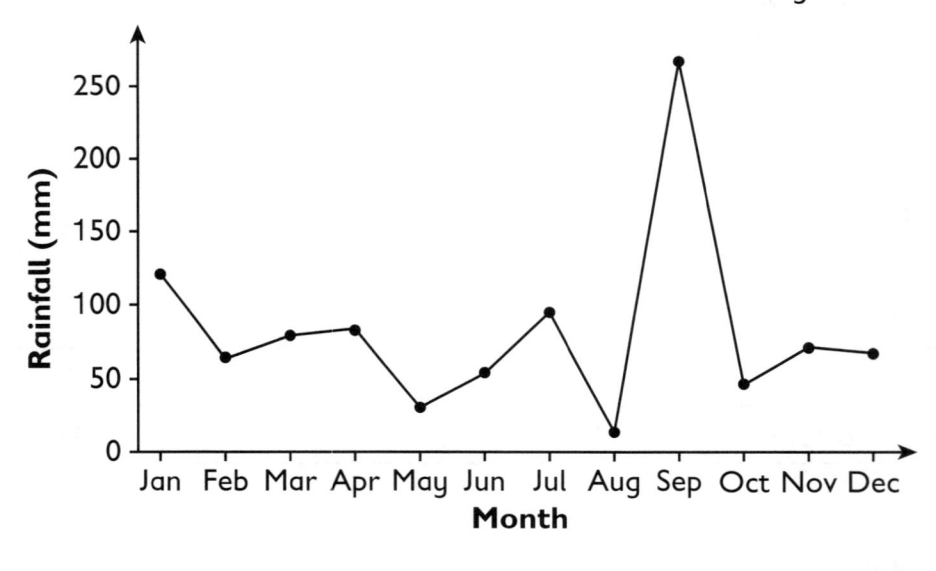

In which month was there the second lowest amount of rainfall?

A	B	C	D	E
August	May	September	January	April

38 Which of these shapes has more than 1 line of symmetry?

A	B	C	D	E
L-shape	teardrop	parallelogram	crescent	rounded square

39 $\frac{1}{5}$ of the fish in a pond have blue scales.

There are 80 fish in the pond that do not have blue scales.

What is the difference between the number of fish that have blue scales and the number of fish that do not have blue scales?

A	B	C	D	E
20	64	40	16	60

40 The height of this triangle is three times greater than its base.

X cm

Which expression shows the area of the triangle?

A	$\left(\frac{X}{2} \times 3X\right)$ cm²
B	$(X \times 3X)$ cm²
C	$\left(\frac{X}{2} \times X\right)$ cm²
D	$\left(\frac{1}{2} \times \frac{X}{2} \times 3X\right)$ cm²
E	$\left(2X \times 3X \times \frac{1}{2}\right)$ cm²

41 What is 4590 shared in 5 equal parts?

A	B	C	D	E
900	915	918	500	480

Questions continue on the next page

42) A restaurant has 25 tables.

20% of the tables can seat 5 people and the rest of the tables can seat 7 people.

What is the maximum number of people that can sit at the tables?

A	B	C	D	E
125 people	175 people	165 people	180 people	140 people

43) A lorry containing 9 boxes of cargo weighs 4582 kg.

Each box of cargo weighs $\frac{1}{5}$ of a tonne.

What is the weight of the lorry and remaining boxes when 7 of the boxes of cargo are removed?

A	B	C	D	E
2782 kg	4582 kg	4382 kg	3549 kg	3182 kg

44) Y is an even number.

Which of the following expressions must be an odd number?

A	B	C	D	E
$Y \div 2$	$8Y + 2$	$3Y - 4$	$Y - 10$	$2Y - 5$

45) Work out the size of the obtuse angle between the hour and minute hands on this clock.

A	B	C	D	E
150°	175°	180°	225°	165°

46) There are three expressions shown below. x is a positive whole number.

What is the difference between the expression with the largest value and the expression with the smallest value?

$x + 7$ $2x + 9$ x

A	B	C	D	E
7	$2x + 7$	$4X + 16$	$3x + 12$	$x + 9$

(47) What fraction of this shape is **not** shaded?

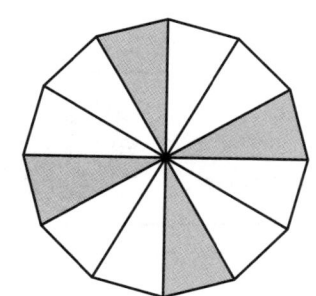

A	B	C	D	E
$\frac{1}{4}$	$\frac{1}{3}$	$\frac{3}{4}$	$\frac{2}{3}$	$\frac{5}{12}$

(48) If $x° = 31°$, what is the value of $b°$?

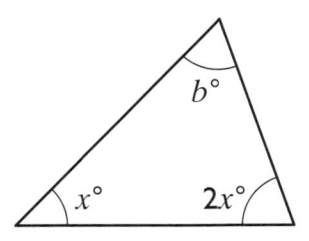

A	B	C	D	E
87°	62°	89°	273°	93°

(49) Mia's mean score in her first 4 tests was 79
Mia's score in her 5th test was 84

What was Mia's mean score in all 5 tests?

A	B	C	D	E
79	82·5	81	80	83

(50) What is the sum of the 3 largest 2-digit prime numbers?

A	B	C	D	E
281	300	269	273	294

Score: ………… / 50

Test 8

You have 50 minutes to complete this test.

You have 50 questions to complete within the given time.

Circle the letter above or alongside the correct answer.

1) What is this number in words?

7007

A	seven thousand and seventy
B	seven thousand, seven hundred
C	seven thousand and seven
D	seventy thousand and seven
E	seven hundred and seventy

2) Rearrange these digits to make the largest number possible.

573 927

A	B	C	D	E
977 532	975 732	235 779	977 352	997 353

3) How many ten-pence coins have the same value as 80 two-pence coins?

A	B	C	D	E
160	90	20	16	32

4) A triangle has a base of 10 cm and a height of 7 cm.

A shape is formed by placing identical versions of the triangle side by side.

The area of the new shape is 210 cm^2.

How many triangles are used to form the new shape?

A	B	C	D	E
6	7	10	15	30

(5) Look at the following train timetable.

Birmingham	0623	0653	0723	0753
Coleshill	0635	0705	0735	0805
Nuneaton	0700	0722	0751	0822
Hinkley	–	0729	0758	0829
Leicester	0717	0748	0817	0848

Jamie takes the 07:23 train from Birmingham to Hinckley.

How long does Jamie's journey take?

A	B	C	D	E
28 minutes	35 minutes	36 minutes	42 minutes	45 minutes

(6) The coordinates of three of the corners of a rectangle have been plotted on the grid below.

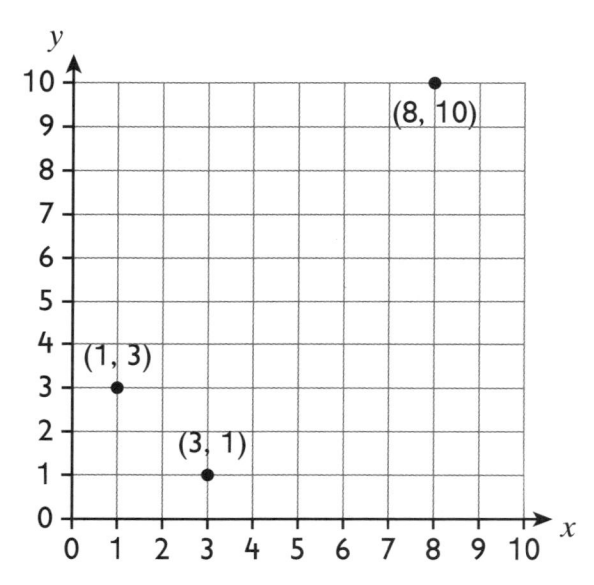

Points shown: (1, 3), (3, 1), (8, 10)

What are the coordinates of the fourth corner of the rectangle?

A	B	C	D	E
(8, 10)	(6, 4)	(7, 9)	(3, 1)	(10, 8)

Questions continue on the next page

(7) How many more factors does the number 36 have than the number 15?

A	B	C	D	E
9	8	5	10	4

(8) Jenny thinks of a decimal number and multiplies it by 4

The answer is a whole number.

Which of the following could be the number that Jenny thought of?

A	B	C	D	E
3·41	3·35	3·85	3·25	3·7

(9) This pictogram shows the hourly wage for different jobs.

Average hourly wage	
Orthodontist	🪙🪙🪙🪙🪙🪙🪙🪙
Lawyer	🪙🪙🪙🪙🪙 ¢
Podiatrist	🪙🪙🪙🪙🪙🪙
Actuary	🪙🪙🪙🪙 ¢
Cashier	🪙

Each 🪙 = £10

Each ¢ = £5

Roy is a lawyer.

He works from 9:00 a.m. to 5:30 p.m. for five days a week.

How much money does Roy earn each week?

A	B	C	D	E
£1657	£275	£2337·50	£55	£2800

10 The average water temperature of a lake is 25% higher than the average for the previous year.

The average water temperature of the lake is 30°C.

What was the average water temperature of the lake for the previous year?

A	B	C	D	E
30°C	24°C	36°C	33°C	26°C

11 Which of these fractions is the smallest?

A	B	C	D	E
$\frac{1}{8}$	$\frac{2}{10}$	$\frac{1}{9}$	$\frac{5}{20}$	$\frac{4}{24}$

12 George faces north.

He makes a quarter turn in a clockwise direction and then turns 135° in an anticlockwise direction.

In which direction does George now face?

A	B	C	D	E
north-east	south-west	north-west	west	south-east

13 The radius of Circle A is 3 times greater than the radius of Circle B.

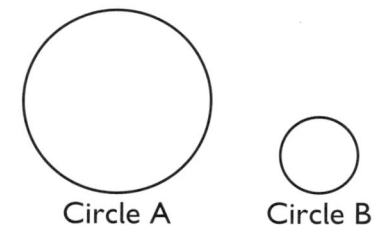

Circle A   Circle B

How many times greater is the radius of Circle A than the diameter of Circle B?

A	B	C	D	E
1 times	$1\frac{1}{2}$ times	2 times	$2\frac{1}{2}$ times	3 times

Questions continue on the next page

14) What is the area of this rectangle?

8.5 cm

2.8 cm

A	B	C	D	E
23·8 cm²	24·6 cm²	25·18 cm²	16·9 cm²	19·4 cm²

15) A farmer feeds each pig on her farm D apples and S turnips per day.

She has 3 dozen pigs on her farm.

Which of the following expressions shows how many apples and turnips the farmer feeds to her pigs in total each week?

A	$36 + 7 + S + D$
B	$36 \times (S + D)$
C	$36 \times 7 \times S \times D$
D	$252D + 252S$
E	$3 \times 12 \times 7 + S \times D$

16) Which of these calculations has the lowest value?

A	$38 + 18 + 14 \times 2$
B	$13 \times 7 + 2 + 19$
C	$43 - 8 + 32 + 80$
D	$12 \times 10 - 5 + 90$
E	$32 - 8 - 6 \times 5$

17) Cube A has a side length of 2 cm.

Cube B has a side length of 4 cm.

What is the percentage increase in volume of Cube B compared to Cube A?

A	B	C	D	E
8%	64%	200%	800%	6400%

18 What value is the arrow pointing to on this number line?

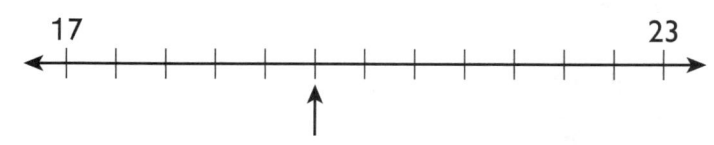

17 23

A	B	C	D	E
19·5	19	21	21·5	20·25

19 400 people took part in a survey.

30% of those who took part were female and the rest were male.

60% of the males who took part were 25 years old or younger.

How many males older than 25 took part in the survey?

A	B	C	D	E
120	168	280	300	112

20 The largest of 5 consecutive even numbers is 18

What is the sum of the 5 numbers?

A	B	C	D	E
140	28	7	70	56

21 Which of these is a reflex angle?

A	B	C	D	E
20°	89°	135°	145°	220°

22 The cost of a coach ticket is £4·40 for an adult and £2·30 for a child.

Mr Jones buys tickets for himself, his wife and his 4 children.

How much does he spend in total?

A	B	C	D	E
£9·20	£6·70	£18·00	£13·60	£8·80

Questions continue on the next page

(23) A bag contains 4 red blocks, 8 green blocks and 7 white blocks.

Sami removes 1 block at random.

What is the probability that the block Sami removes is **not** green?

A	B	C	D	E
$\frac{1}{20}$	$\frac{8}{19}$	$\frac{11}{19}$	$\frac{14}{19}$	$\frac{5}{11}$

(24) What fraction of this shape is shaded?

A	B	C	D	E
$\frac{3}{10}$	$\frac{1}{9}$	$\frac{6}{9}$	$\frac{1}{3}$	$\frac{4}{5}$

(25) The ratio of lions, tigers and leopards in a jungle is 4:3:8

If there are 78 tigers in the jungle, how many leopards are there?

A	B	C	D	E
26	156	208	39	234

(26) Cube A is formed from identical smaller cubes, each with a side length of 2 cm.

What is the volume of Cube A?

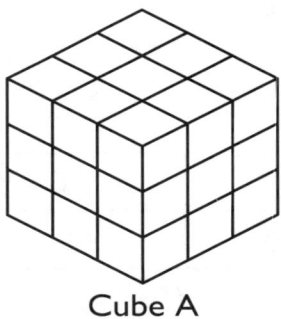

Cube A

A	B	C	D	E
8 cm³	54 cm³	64 cm³	27 cm³	216 cm³

27) Set A consists of all numbers greater than 7 but less than 48

Set B consists of all multiples of 6

How many numbers appear in both Set A and Set B?

A	B	C	D	E
3	4	5	6	7

28) Tamara wants to calculate the distance from London to Paris.

Which of the following would be the most appropriate unit of measurement for her to use?

A	B	C	D	E
mm	cm	m	km	kg

29) What is the value of $B°$?

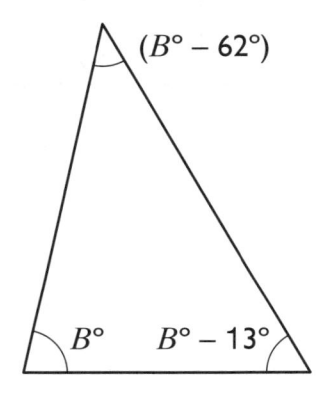

Triangle with angles $B°$, $B° - 13°$, and $(B° - 62°)$

A	B	C	D	E
90°	82°	85°	78°	57°

30) It takes 7 people 21 hours to build a fence.

How long would it take 21 people to build the same fence?

A	B	C	D	E
14 hours	21 hours	147 hours	12 hours	7 hours

31) 6·7 km ÷ 8 =

A	B	C	D	E
900·5 m	845 m	837·5 m	820 m	810 m

Questions continue on the next page

(32) Which of these shapes has an order of rotational symmetry of 2?

A	B	C	D	E
square	triangle	rhombus	heart	pentagon

(33) Which line is perpendicular to line X?

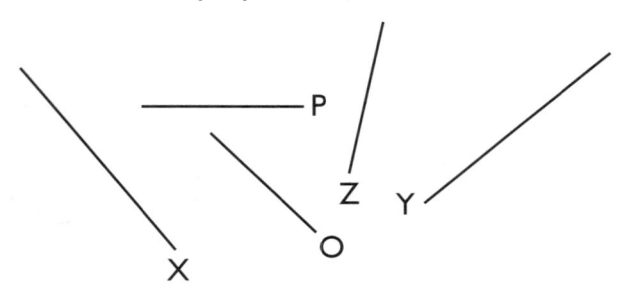

A	B	C	D	E
O	P	X	Y	Z

(34) There are 9 warehouses in a factory.
Each warehouse holds 54 crates.
Each crate holds 19 robots.

How many robots are there in the factory?
Round your answer to the nearest 10

A	B	C	D	E
9240	1030	2500	9230	1020

(35) A jar contains 12 red sweets, 13 blue sweets, 11 green sweets and 10 yellow sweets.

Which of these statements is **false**?

A	There are more red sweets than yellow sweets in the jar.
B	There are more blue sweets than red sweets in the jar.
C	There are more green sweets than yellow sweets in the jar.
D	There are more yellow sweets than blue sweets in the jar.
E	There are more blue sweets than red sweets in the jar.

36 Which of these numbers is closest to 0·3?

A	B	C	D	E
0·305	0·31	0·298	0·2	0·2002

37 The mean number of cakes eaten by the people at an event was $2\frac{3}{4}$.

If there were 20 people at the event, how many cakes were eaten in total?

A	B	C	D	E
15 cakes	20 cakes	40 cakes	55 cakes	60 cakes

38 What percentage of 1 year is 54 months?

A	B	C	D	E
3%	22%	4·50%	450%	80%

39 If b is an odd number, which of the following must be an even number?

A	B	C	D	E
$b - 8$	$2b$	$3b$	$2b - 5$	$b + 2$

40 A car travels at a speed of 100 kph for 4 hours.
It then does not move for 1 hour.
Finally, it travels 3 hours at a speed of 70 kph.

What is the car's average speed over this whole period?

A	B	C	D	E
100 kph	70 kph	76.25 kph	21.25 kph	85 kph

41 Andrew mixes 2 litres of squash with 4 times as much water.

How many 200 ml cups can he fill with this mixture?

A	B	C	D	E
30 cups	50 cups	40 cups	20 cups	10 cups

Questions continue on the next page

42) Parv drew a shape in which the internal angles add up to 360°.

Which of these shapes could Parv have drawn?

A	B	C	D	E
triangle	rhombus	pentagon	hexagon	octagon

43) The mean of 8, 9, A and B is 10

What is the sum of A and B?

A	B	C	D	E
40	3	23	17	10

44) Which number comes next in this sequence?

18 21 25 30 36 ?

A	B	C	D	E
40	45	54	60	43

45) The coordinates of two corners of a square on a centimetre grid are (−5, 7) and (3, −1).

What is the area of the square?

A	B	C	D	E
8 cm²	64 cm²	60 cm²	100 cm²	36 cm²

46) A dice was rolled 100 times.

The frequency of each score was recorded in this pie chart.

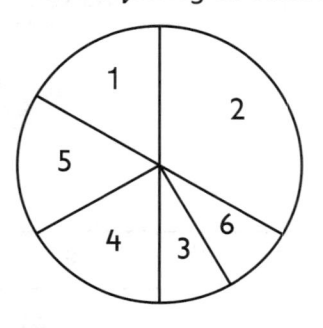

What was the most common score?

A	B	C	D	E
1	2	6	5	4

47 The ratio of the number of oranges to the number of bananas in a box is 7:6

Which of the following could **not** be the total number of oranges and bananas in the box?

A	B	C	D	E
26	78	64	117	104

48 How many different combinations of coins can have a total of 10 pence?

A	B	C	D	E
3	6	8	10	11

49 This graph shows the distance covered by a cyclist on a trip.

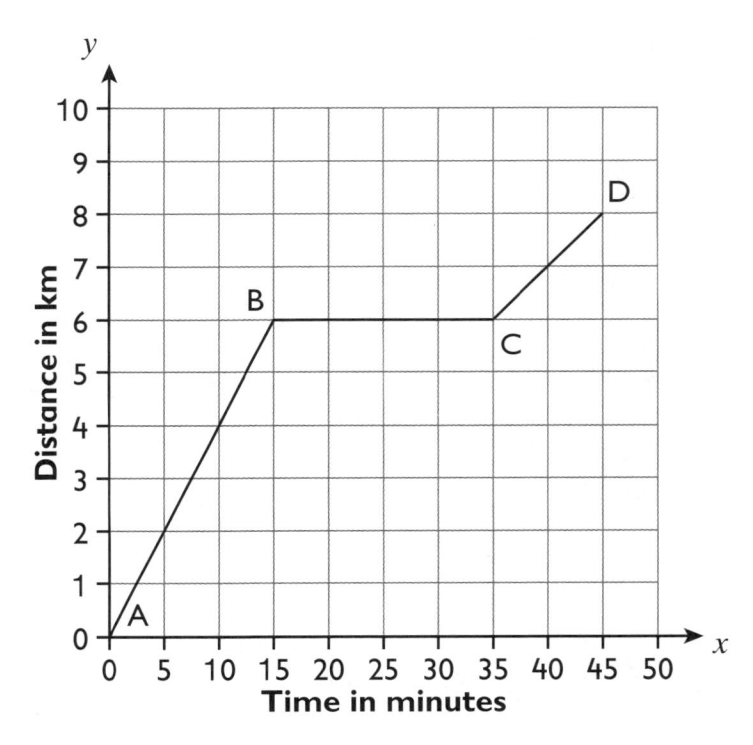

For how long was the cyclist stationary during the trip?

A	B	C	D	E
0 minutes	10 minutes	15 minutes	20 minutes	25 minutes

Questions continue on the next page

50 What is the perimeter of this shape?

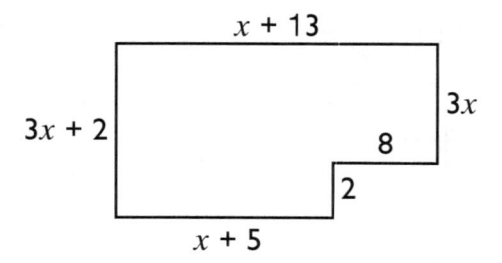

```
         x + 13
      ┌─────────┐
3x + 2│         │ 3x
      │      ┌──┘
      │      │ 8
      │      │2
      └──────┘
        x + 5
```

A	$4x + 15$
B	$3x + 15$
C	$8x + 30$
D	$3x + 2 + x + 13 + 3x + 8 + 2 + x + 6$
E	$2x + 18$

Score: .... / 50

Maths dictionary

Acute: an angle less than 90°

Adjacent: next to; the side next to the angle that is being worked on in a triangle (not the hypotenuse)

Allied angles: angles formed when a line crosses a pair of parallel lines; allied angles add up to 180°, i.e. $a + b = 180°$

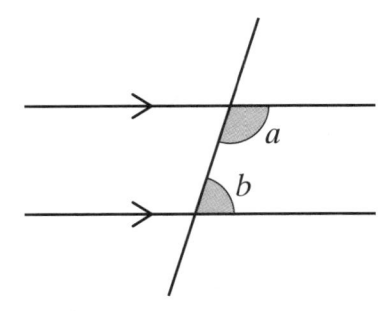

Alternate angles: angles formed when a line crosses a pair of parallel lines; alternate angles are equal, i.e. $a = b$

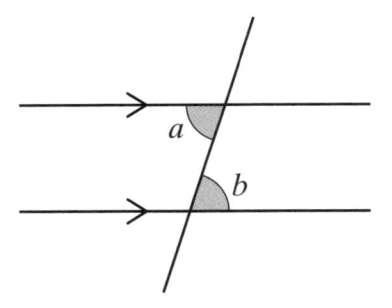

Angles at a point: angles at a point add up to 360°, i.e. $a + b + c + d = 360°$

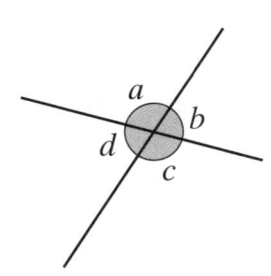

Angles in a triangle: angles in a triangle add up to 180°, i.e. $a + b + c = 180°$

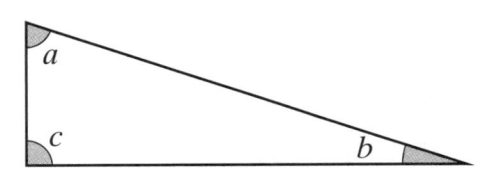

Angles on a straight line: The angles at a point on a straight line add up to 180°, i.e. $a + b = 180°$

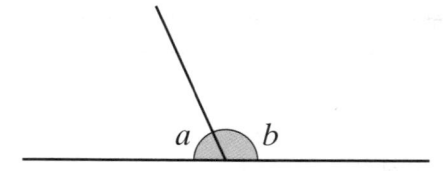

Area: the amount of space inside the perimeter of a 2D shape, measured in unit squares, e.g. cm²

Arithmetic sequence: a sequence of numbers with a common difference between each term and the next

Circumference: the perimeter of a circle

Cone: a 3D shape that tapers from a circular base to a point (a pyramid with a circular base)

Congruent: the same size and shape

Continuous data: data that can take any value within a given range, e.g. length or time

Corresponding angles: angles formed when a line crosses a pair of parallel lines; corresponding angles are equal, i.e. $a = b$

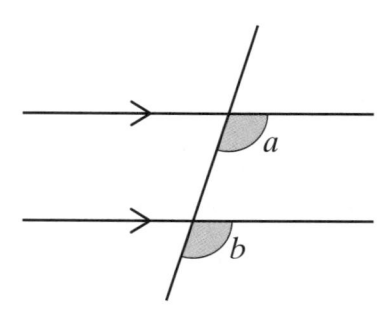

Cube number: the product of multiplying a number by itself three times, e.g. $4 \times 4 \times 4 = 4^3 = 64$

Decimal places (d.p.): the number of digits after the decimal point

Denominator: the bottom number of a fraction

Density: the ratio of mass to volume

Direct proportion: two values or measurements that remain in the same ratio; when one value increases, then so does the other

Discrete data: data that can only take certain values in a given range, e.g. number of goals scored

Edge: the line where two faces of 3D shape meet

Enlargement: to make bigger whilst retaining the original shape

Equation: a number sentence where one side is equal to the other

Equilateral: a triangle with three equal sides and three equal angles (60°)

Equivalent: the same as

Estimate: an approximate value (often made by rounding the numbers in a calculation to 1 significant figure)

Expand (brackets): to remove brackets from an expression by multiplication

Expression: an algebraic statement that uses numbers and letters

Exterior: outside

Face: a flat surface or side of a 3D shape

Factor (divisor): a number that will divide exactly into another

Formula / formulae (pl.): a rule that is expressed as an equation; often used in science

Fraction: part of a whole

Highest common factor (HCF): the largest positive integer that will divide exactly into two numbers

Hypotenuse: the longest side of a right-angled triangle; opposite the right angle

Improper fraction: a fraction with a numerator that is greater than its denominator

Inequality: a linear expression showing two quantities that are not equal; symbols used are $>$, $\geqslant$, $<$, $\leqslant$

Interior: inside

Inverse operation: the opposite operation, e.g. subtraction is the opposite operation to addition and division is opposite to multiplication

Inverse proportion: as one quantity increases, the other quantity decreases

Irregular: shapes in which some of the sides and angles are unequal

Isosceles: a triangle with two equal sides and two equal angles

Kite: a quadrilateral in which two pairs of adjacent sides are equal

Linear equation: an equation that does not contain any variables over the power of 1, e.g. $x = 2y + 3$

Lower bound: the lower limit of a rounded number

Lowest common multiple (LCM): the lowest integer which is a multiple of both numbers

Mean: an average found by dividing the sum of all values by the number of values

Median: the middle value when the values in a data set are put in order

Mixed number: contains a whole number and a fraction

Mode: the most frequently occurring value in a data set

Multiples: the multiples of a number appear in its 'times table'

Multiplier: the number by which another number is multiplied; a decimal multiplier can be used in percentage change calculations

Negative numbers: all numbers less than 0; shown using a minus symbol (–)

Numerator: the top number of a fraction

nth term: the general term of a number sequence

Obtuse: an angle between 90° and 180°

Opposite side: the side opposite the angle that is being worked on in a triangle

Parallel: two or more lines that run in the same direction and are always the same distance apart

Parallelogram: a quadrilateral in which opposite sides are equal and parallel

Percentage: out of one hundred

Perimeter: the boundary of a shape; the length of that boundary

Perpendicular: a line at 90° to another line

Polygon: a closed shape bounded by straight lines

Power: a small digit to the top right of a number that shows the number of times by which the number is to be multiplied by itself, e.g. $4^2 = 4 \times 4$ and $4^3 = 4 \times 4 \times 4$

Prime factor: a prime number that is also a factor; numbers can be broken down into their prime factors to help find common factors and multiples

Prime number: a number that has only two factors, itself and 1

Probability: a measure of the how likely it is that an event or outcome will happen; can be expressed as a fraction, decimal or percentage

Proportion: describes the relationship between things or the parts of something, in terms of their comparative sizes or quantities

Pyramid: a 3D shape in which lines drawn from the vertices of the base meet at a point

Pythagoras' theorem: a theorem that states that the square on the hypotenuse of a right-angled triangle is equal to the sum of the squares on the other two sides, i.e. $a^2 + b^2 = c^2$

Quadrilateral: a four-sided shape

Quotient: the result of dividing one number by another, e.g. in 12 ÷ 4 = 3, the quotient is 3

Radius / radii (pl.): the length of a straight line from the centre of a circle to its circumference

Random: when each object / person has an equal chance of being selected

Range: the spread of data; found by subtracting the smallest value from the greatest value

Ratio: the relative amounts of two or more things, shown in the form A : B

Rational number: a number that can be written exactly in fraction or decimal form e.g. $\frac{1}{4} = 0.25$

Recurring: repeating

Reflection: a transformation that produces a mirror image of the original object

Reflex: an angle between 180° and 360°

Regular: a shape in which all the sides are equal and all the angles are equal

Rhombus: a quadrilateral in which all sides are equal and opposite sides are parallel

Root: a root is the inverse operation to an index or power, e.g. $\sqrt{x}$ is the inverse of x^2 and $\sqrt[3]{x}$ is the inverse of x^3

Rotation: a transformation that turns an object; every point of the object is turned through the same angle about a given point

Scale factor: the ratio by which an object is made bigger or smaller

Scalene: a triangle with no equal sides or equal angles

Sequence: a collection of terms that follow a rule or pattern

Significant figures: a means of approximating numbers; the first significant figure is the first non-zero figure (working from left to right)

Similar: similar figures are identical in shape but differ in size

Simplify: to make simpler, usually by cancelling down

Simultaneous equations: two equations that are true at the same time (the different variables have the same values in both equations) and can therefore be solved together

Speed: a measure of how fast something is moving, i.e. $\frac{\text{distance}}{\text{time}}$

Sphere: A 3D shape that is round, like a ball; at every point, its surface is equidistant from its centre

Square number: the result of multiplying a number by itself, e.g. $4^2 = 4 \times 4 = 16$

Square root: the inverse of a square number, e.g. $4^2 = 16$ and $\sqrt{16} = 4$

Standard form: a number written in the form $a \times 10^n$, where a is a number between 1 and 10; for large numbers n is positive and for small numbers n is negative

Term: in an expression, any of the quantities connected to each other by an addition or subtraction sign; in a sequence, any of the values connected to each other by a pattern or rule

Transformation: an action that brings about a change to the position, size or orientation of a shape, i.e. translation, rotation, reflection and/or enlargement

Translation: a transformation that moves the object, but does not turn it

Trapezium: a quadrilateral with one pair of parallel sides

Upper bound: the upper limit of a rounded number

Variable: a quantity that can have many values; often written as a letter

Vertex / vertices (pl.): the corner of a shape

Volume: the amount of space occupied by a substance or enclosed within a container, measured in unit cubes, e.g. cm^3

Answers

Key abbreviations:

°C	degrees Celsius
m	metre
cm	centimetre
mm	millimetre
km	kilometre
kg	kilogram
ml	millilitre
kph	kilometres per hour
d.p.	decimal places

TEST 1

Q1 B

Thousands	Hundreds	Tens	Ones
9	8	4	2

Q2 C
The rule is 'add 8' each time.
Missing number = 571 + 8 = 579

Q3 D
Number of rectangles that fit left to right:
32 m ÷ 16 m = 2
Number of rectangles that fit top to bottom:
32 m ÷ 8 m = 4
Number of rectangles to fill square = 2 × 4 = 8

Q4 D
7 cm ÷ 100 = 0·07 m
Garth's height = 1·32 m + 0·07 m = 1·39 m

Q5 E
Shape consists of 10 identical squares, 4 of which are shaded.
Fraction shaded = $\frac{4}{10} = \frac{2}{5}$

Q6 D
7453 ÷ X = 7453
Any number divided by 1 equals itself, so X = 1

Q7 A
a + 8 = 17 + 15
a + 8 = 32
$\quad a$ = 32 − 8 = 24

Q8 C
Number of weeks = £60 ÷ £7·50 = 8

Q9 D
Groups that contain more than 20 students:
B, C, D, E, H, I, J
7 groups contain more than 20 students.

Q10 D
Diameter = 2 × radius
Radius of Circle A = 2 × diameter of Circle B
$\qquad\qquad\qquad$ = 4 × radius of Circle B
Diameter of Circle A = 2 × 4 × radius of Circle B
$\qquad\qquad\qquad\quad$ = 8 × radius of Circle B
The diameter of Circle A is 8 times greater than the radius of Circle B.

TEST 2

Q1 C
Time spent working on Project 3 per day =
25% of 8 hours = 2 hours
Time spent working on Project 3 in one week =
2 hours × 7 = 14 hours

Q2 E
$2\frac{1}{3}$ hours = 2 hours 20 minutes
2 hours 20 minutes after 3·40 p.m. is 6.00 p.m.

Q3 C
Speed = 600 km ÷ 15 hours = 40 kph

Q4 D
35 ÷ ❖ = 21·6 − 4·1
35 ÷ ❖ = 17·5
❖ = 35 ÷ 17·5 = 2

Q5 D
A pentagon has 5 sides.
Shape D has 6 sides.

Q6 A
Cost of 10 tiles = £3·50 ÷ 2 = £1·75
Cost of 70 tiles = £1·75 × 7 = £12·25

Q7 B
The 17:42 train from Derayston arrives at Baldington at 18:56
It is the only train that arrives at Baldington before 19:00

Q8 D
60 is larger than 40, so the answer will be greater than 100%.
40 = 100%, 20 = 50%, so 60 = 100 + 50 = 150%
OR
$\frac{60}{40}$ × 100 = 1·5 × 100 = 150%

Q9 D
The question asks for the saving per ticket not the total saving.
Saving per ticket = 10% of £8·20 = £0·82

Q10 D
Angle A is between 90° (a right angle) and 180° (a straight line), so it is obtuse.

TEST 3

Q1 A
8272·6 ÷ 100 = 82·726

Q2 B
Number of apples sold = $\frac{1}{3}$ of 750 = 250
Number of apples remaining = 750 − 250 = 500
Number of apples thrown away = 500 ÷ 2 = 250
Number of apples left in cart = 500 − 250 = 250

Q3 B
Number of days in August = 31
Number of cups processed = 31 × 671 = 20 801

Test 3 answers continue on next page

Q4 **C**

The differences between the numbers in the sequence are:

+1, + 4, + 9, + 16…

These are the first four square numbers.

Next square number = 25

Next number in sequence = 45 + 25 = 70

Q5 **A**

10% of 231 kg = 23·1 kg

Weight this year = 231 kg + 23·1 kg = 254·1 kg

Q6 **E**

The spring temperature is higher than the winter temperature, so you must add.

Average spring temperature = −14°C + 9·5°C = −4·5°C

Q7 **C**

You can convert the fractions to decimals to make the comparison:

$\frac{1}{4}$ = 0·25, $\frac{1}{8}$ = 0·125, $\frac{3}{4}$ = 0·75, $\frac{5}{8}$ = 0·525, $\frac{3}{9}$ = 0·333…,

$\frac{8}{10}$ = 0·8

Starting from smallest: 0·125, 0·25, 0·333…, 0·525, 0·75, 0·8

Convert back to fractions: $\frac{1}{8}$ $\frac{1}{4}$ $\frac{3}{9}$ $\frac{5}{8}$ $\frac{3}{4}$ $\frac{8}{10}$

Q8 **B**

36 is the only option that is an even number, a square number and a multiple of 9

Q9 **A**

7·622 + 13·329 = 20·951

Q10 **C**

The scale increases by 0·2 each time, so the marks show 4·4, 4·6, 4·8, 5·0

4·7 is halfway between the marks showing 4·6 and 4·8

The arrow pointing to the halfway point is C.

Q11 **C**

When reflecting in the x-axis, the x-coordinate (first number) stays the same.

The y-coordinate (second number) changes from positive to negative or from negative to positive.

So the coordinates of Point C are (5, 8).

Q12 **D**

The number in the box must be 10 times smaller than 242 676

242 676 ÷ 10 = 24 267·6

Q13 **C**

421 ÷ 52 = 8 Remainder 5

Therefore, 9 buses will be needed in total to carry all the passengers.

Q14 **D**

48 × 7 + 4 = 223 + X

336 + 4 = 223 + X

340 = 223 + X

340 − 223 = X

117 = X

Q15 **E**

64 cm³ = 4 cm × 4 cm × 4 cm

Side length of Cube A = 4 cm

Area of one face of Cube A = 4 cm × 4 cm = 16 cm²

Q16 **D**

Number of edges = 18

Number of faces = 8

Difference = 18 − 8 = 10

Q17 **D**

Length of Cuboid B = 7 cm × 2 = 14 cm

Width of Cuboid B = 3 cm × 2 = 6 cm

Height of Cuboid B = 4 cm × 3 = 12 cm

Volume of Cuboid B = 14 cm × 6 cm × 12 cm = 1008 cm³

Q18 **D**

247 ÷ 13 = 19

Q19 **B**

100 apples represent 5 parts.

1 part = 100 ÷ 5 = 20

Number of peaches = 7 × 20 = 140

Number of bananas = 3 × 20 = 60

Difference = 140 − 60 = 80

Q20 **B**

Mean weight = $\frac{\text{total weight of turnips}}{\text{number of turnips}}$

So, total weight of turnips = number of turnips × mean weight

Total weight of 5 turnips = 5 × 4·5 kg = 22·5 kg

Total weight of 6 turnips = 6 × 4·6 kg = 27·6 kg

Weight of added turnip = 27·6 kg − 22·5 kg = 5·1 kg

TEST 4

Q1 **D**

£3·60 = 360p

Number of coins = 360p ÷ 20p = 18

Q2 **A**

The question asks for the largest *percentage* increase.

The largest increase in population is between 2010 and 2011.

However, this only represents growth of roughly $\frac{1}{3}$ from 2010, so around 33%.

From 2005 to 2006, the population increases by roughly $3\frac{1}{2}$ times, so around 350%.

This is clearly the largest *percentage* increase between two years.

Q3 **B**

Length of 1 side = 40·2 cm ÷ 6 = 6·7 cm

Length of 2 sides = 6·7 cm × 2 = 13·4 cm

Q4 **D**

Smallest number (digits arranged from smallest to largest) = 23 889

Second smallest number = 23 898

Q5 **E**

Landing in London time: $11\frac{1}{2}$ hours after 2·30 p.m. → 2·00 a.m.

Landing in Hong Kong time: 8 hours after 2·00 a.m. → 10·00 a.m.

The options are given as 24-hour clock times.

10·00 a.m. is 10:00

Q6 **D**

The side length of the square is 6 units, so the coordinates of Point C are (2, −2).

Q7 A

Hundred thousands	Ten thousands	Thousands	Hundreds	Tens	Ones
4	0	0	0	1	9

Q8 E

$7\frac{3}{4} = 7\frac{6}{8}$

Number of eighths = $(7 \times 8) + 6 = 56 + 6 = 62$

Q9 E

$3600 \div 18 = 200$

Q10 D

Sixteen of the small squares would fit into the large square.

One is shaded, so the fraction shaded is $\frac{1}{16}$

OR

$\frac{1}{4}$ of $\frac{1}{4}$ of the square is shaded, so fraction shaded = $\frac{1}{4} \times \frac{1}{4} = \frac{1}{16}$

Q11 E

Hundreds	Tens	Ones	•	Tenths	Hundredths	Thousandths
4	5	6	•	7	8	3

Q12 C

Total number of doughnuts eaten = $(6 \times 6) + (4 \times 4) = 36 + 16 = 52$

Total number of children = $6 + 4 = 10$

Mean = $\frac{52}{10} = 5\cdot2$

5·2 rounded to the nearest whole number is 5

Q13 D

$\frac{15}{45} = \frac{1}{3}$

$\frac{1}{3} = \frac{20}{60}$, so $\triangle = 60$

Q14 B

Total spent = $(£110 \div 2) + £7\cdot50 + £7\cdot50 + £4\cdot50$
= $£55 + £7\cdot50 + £7\cdot50 + £4\cdot50 = £74\cdot50$

Money left = $£110 - £74\cdot50 = £35\cdot50$

Q15 B

Buses in April, July and August = $24 \times 10 = 240$

Q16 C

She cuts the ribbon in half, so she has 2 pieces.

Each of these halves is cut into 7 pieces.

Number of pieces = $2 \times 7 = 14$

Q17 D

Angles in a triangle add up to 180°.

Size of third angle = $180° - 75° - 18° = 87°$

Q18 A

The differences between the numbers in the sequence are:

$-10, ?, ?, -7, -6$

So, the pattern is:

$-10, -9, -8, -7, -6$

Missing number = $35 - 9 = 26$

Q19 B

$(48 - 7) \times 3 = 41 \times 3 = 123$

Q20 C

The arrow points to 800 ml.

800 ml $\div$ 1000 = 0·8 litres

TEST 5

Q1 D

$486 \div 9 = 54$

Q2 C

1·5 litres $\div$ 0·5 litre = 3

OR

1·5 litres = 0·5 litre + 0·5 litre + 0·5 litre, so 1·5 litres is 3 times greater than 0·5 litre

Q3 E

Number of blue stamps = $\frac{1}{3}$ of $336 = 336 \div 3 = 112$

Number of stamps that are not blue = $336 - 112 = 224$

OR

Number of stamps that are not blue = $\frac{2}{3}$ of $336 = 224$

Q4 D

Total cost = $£25\cdot50 \times 4 = £102\cdot00$

Amount needed = $£102\cdot00 - £18\cdot00 = £84\cdot00$

Q5 D

$0\cdot65 - 0\cdot6 = 0\cdot05$

$0\cdot6 - 0\cdot58 = 0\cdot02$

$0\cdot6 - 0\cdot585 = 0\cdot015$

$0\cdot601 - 0\cdot6 = 0\cdot001$

$0\cdot61001 - 0\cdot6 = 0\cdot01001$

0·001 is the smallest difference, 0·601 is closest to 0·6

Q6 A

Compare the digits in the tenths column and then compare the digits in the hundredths column.

0·715   0·175   0·164   0·158

Q7 C

Cost of 1 lemon = $£1\cdot56 \div 3 = £0\cdot52$

Cost of 7 lemons = $£0\cdot52 \times 7 = £3\cdot64$

Q8 E

120% of 35 = $1\cdot2 \times 35 = 42$

OR

100% = 35

20% = $\frac{1}{5}$ of $35 = 35 \div 5 = 7$

120% = $35 + 7 = 42$

Q9 E

Length = $7\cdot5$ cm $\times 2 = 15$ cm

Perimeter = 15 cm + 7·5 cm + 15 cm + 7·5 cm = 45 cm

Q10 D

There were more visitors from Brazil than from Sweden, so D is false.

Q11 D

$1\frac{3}{4}$ hours = 1 hour 45 minutes

1 hour and 45 minutes before 2·21 p.m. is 12·36 p.m.

Q12 D

$\frac{2}{3}$ of $B = \frac{2}{3}$ of $60 = 40$

$\frac{4}{5}$ of $A = 40$

$\frac{1}{5}$ of $A = 40 \div 4 = 10$

$A = 10 \times 5 = 50$

Q13 D

Arrow 4 points anticlockwise.

All the other arrows point clockwise.

So, rotating arrow 4 will not produce arrow 2

Q14 E

Radius = 15·5 cm $\div 2 = 7\cdot75$ cm

Test 5 answers continue on next page

Q15 B
Total spent per month = £550 + £225 = £775
Total spent per year = £775 × 12 = £9300

Q16 A
Angles on a straight line add up to 180°.
So, the two angles at the foot of the triangle are:
180° − 138° = 42°
180° − 136° = 44°
Angles in a triangle add up to 180°.
So, Angle D = 180° − 42° − 44° = 94°

Q17 A
Total distance = 8 + 6 + 8 + 10 + 10 = 42 km
45 minutes = $\frac{3}{4}$ of an hour
Distance covered in $\frac{1}{4}$ of an hour = 42 km ÷ 3 = 14 km
Distance covered in 1 hour = 14 km × 4 = 56 km
The average speed is 56 kph.

Q18 C
Weight of rubbish = 420 kg − 102·5 kg = 317·5 kg

Q19 E
Total number of grapes picked
= 1348 + 2311 + 3213 + 2568 = 9440
Mean number of grapes picked per day
= 9440 ÷ 5 = 1888
Mean number of grapes picked per worker
= 1888 ÷ 4 = 472

Q20 B
The shape has 16 sides, each measuring 5 cm.
Perimeter = 16 × 5 cm = 80 cm

Q21 B
$2s + 4b = 81$
$(2 × 0·5) + 4b = 81$
$1 + 4b = 81$
$4b = 81 − 1$
$4b = 80$
$b = 80 ÷ 4$
$b = 20$

Q22 B
Volume = height × width × length
250 = 10 × 5 × length
250 = 50 × length
Length = 250 ÷ 50 = 5 cm

Q23 E
Work backwards using inverse operations:
10·5 + 17 = 27·5
27·5 − 8 = 19·5
19·5 × 2 = 39

Q24 B
Height = 5 cm × 3 = 15 cm
Area of triangle = $\frac{1}{2}$ × base × height
= $\frac{1}{2}$ × 5 cm × 15 cm = 37·5 cm²

Q25 A
Total cost = £4·65 + £4·65 + £0·55 = £9·85
Change received = £10·00 − £9·85 = £0·15

Q26 D
0·0282 + 2·7301 = 2·7583

Q27 C
The lines on two sides of the triangle show that they are equal length.
Therefore, the triangle is isosceles (two equal sides and two equal angles).
The angles in a triangle add up to 180°.
So, Angle H = (180° − 90°) ÷ 2 = 45°

Q28 D
The graph doesn't extend to £16, so look for a factor of 16
£8 = €5
So, £16 = €5 × 2 = €10

Q29 A
8·47 a.m. → 4·17 p.m. is 7 hours and 30 minutes or $7\frac{1}{2}$ hours

Q30 B
Difference = highest score − lowest score
= 98 − 14 = 84

TEST 6

Q1 D
45·6508
The fourth digit after the decimal point is greater than 5, so round up.
45·651 rounded to 3 d.p.

Q2 D
The expression must be in pence
£10·00 × 100 = 1000 p
Cost of 3 chocolate bars = 3 × y = 3y
Change received = 1000 − 3y

Q3 D
Perpendicular means 'at right-angles to'.
The line from (0, 0) to (5, −5) is at a right-angle to the line in the diagram.

Q4 D
$1·65 = \frac{165}{100} = \frac{33}{20}$

Q5 B
Width = 6b ÷ 3 = 2b
Perimeter = 6b + 2b + 6b + 2b = 16b

Q6 B
1 is both a square number and a cube number.

Q7 D
£85 = 85% of original price
Original price = $\left(\frac{£85}{85}\right)$ × 100 = £100

Q8 D
Cost of 3 lemons = 32 p × 3 = 96 p = cost of 2 oranges
Cost of 4 oranges = 96 p × 2 = 192 p = cost of 8 pears
Cost of 4 pears = 192 p ÷ 2 = 96 p

Q9 B
Number of tiles that fit along the length
= 6 m ÷ 0·5 m = 12
Number of tiles that fit along the width
= 2·5 m ÷ 0·5 m = 5
Total number of tiles to cover the floor = 12 × 5 = 60

Q10 B
$3y + 5 = (3 × 4) + 5 = 17$
$4y + 6 = (4 × 4) + 6 = 22$
$4y − 1 = (4 × 4) − 1 = 15$
Mean = $\frac{\text{sum of all values}}{\text{number of values}}$
= $\frac{17 + 22 + 15}{3} = \frac{54}{3} = 18$

Q11 **A**
Total length = 25 m + 1 m + 1 m = 27 m
Total width = 10 m + 1 m + 1 m = 12 m
27 m × 12 m = 324 m²

Q12 **E**
The sum of all the angles in a square is
(90° + 90° + 90° + 90° =) 360°

Q13 **D**
10% increase = £10 000
So the initial amount = $\frac{£10\,000}{10} \times 100$ = £100 000
Number of shares = £100 000 ÷ £50 = 2000

Q14 **E**
The ratio of bananas to oranges is 7:4
132 oranges represent 4 parts
1 part = 132 ÷ 4 = 33
Number of bananas = 33 × 7 = 231

Q15 **C**
Amount received = £4·80 ÷ 3 = £1·60

Q16 **C**
Volume = width × length × height
It is a cube, so all side lengths are the same.
125 cm³ = 5 cm × 5 cm × 5 cm
Area of 1 face = width × length
= 5 cm × 5 cm = 25 cm²
A cube has 6 faces.
Total surface area = 25 cm² × 6 = 150 cm²

Q17 **C**
270° anticlockwise is a $\frac{3}{4}$ turn left, so he would face north-east.

Q18 **E**
Number of sides = 4 × 5 = 20
Perimeter = 7·5 cm × 20 = 150 cm

Q19 **A**
1·7 × 0·04 = 0·068

Q20 **D**
315 ÷ 9 = 35
315 ÷ 5 = 63
315 ÷ 4 = 78·75
315 is a multiple of 9 and 5, but not of 4

Q21 **B**
33 × 110 = 3630
3630 − 3200 = 430

Q22 **D**
The angles at a point (at the centre of a circle) add up to 360°.
25% = $\frac{1}{4}$
$\frac{1}{4}$ of 360° = 360° ÷ 4 = 90°

Q23 **D**
The angles in a triangle add up to 180°.
$X° + 5X° + 4X° = 180°$
$10X° = 180°$
$X° = 180° ÷ 10$
$X° = 18°$
$2X° = 18° × 2 = 36°$

Q24 **E**
There are 12 other children in the queue.
There are twice as many in front of Maria as there are behind.
12 ÷ 3 = 4
So, there are (4 × 2 =) 8 in front and 4 behind her.
She is 9th.

Q25 **E**
4 out of 10 balls are striped
$\frac{4}{10} = \frac{2}{5}$

Q26 **A**
Temperature on Friday = −20° + 3° = −17°
Temperature on Saturday = −17° − 7° = −24°

Q27 **E**
Amount of water used = 450 ml × 4·5 = 2025 ml
2025 ml = 2·025 litres
Amount of water left = 3·500 litres − 2·025 litres
= 1·475 litres

Q28 **B**
−15 → 25 is 40
40 ÷ 2 = 20
−15 + 20 = 5

Q29 **C**
33 − 11 − 5 = 17

Q30 **C**
1 fortnight = 2 weeks
2 weeks out of 7 weeks = $\frac{2}{7}$

TEST 7

Q1 **D**
Number of eighths = 12 × 8 = 96

Q2 **D**
2450 rounded to the nearest 100 = 2500
2366 rounded to the nearest 50 = 2350
2458 rounded to the nearest 10 = 2460
2445 rounded to the nearest 10 = **2450**
2480 rounded to the nearest 10 = 2480

Q3 **B**
Sam's bar is the tallest for March.

Q4 **B**
Put the digits in order, from largest to smallest: 87 321

Q5 **D**
$5\frac{1}{2}$ hours earlier than 02:45 is 21:15

Q6 **A**
Angle A is acute (less than 90° / a right angle).
20° is the best estimate.

Q7 **E**
49 + (18 ÷ 6)
= 49 + 3 = 52

Q8 **D**
4·8 litres = 4800 ml
Number of bottles = 4800 ml ÷ 300 ml = 16

Q9 **E**
37·5% = $\frac{3}{8}$
$\frac{1}{8}$ of 80 = 80 ÷ 8 = 10
$\frac{3}{8}$ of 80 = 10 × 3 = 30

Test 7 answers continue on next page

Q10 E
The other moves are either rotations and/or enlargements

Q11 E
Shortest route = 250 m + 250 m + 250 m = 750 m
750 m ÷ 1000 = 0·75 km

Q12 A
Work backwards:
120 ÷ 2 = 60
75 − 60 = 15

Q13 C
Total weight of 3 boxes = 3 × 3·45 kg = 10·35 kg
Weight of 3rd box = 10·35 kg − 3·5 kg − 3·5 kg = 3·35 kg

Q14 A
Point B is on the y-axis, so its x-coordinate must be 0

Q15 A
45° or a $\frac{1}{8}$ turn clockwise from south-west is west.

Q16 D
80 kg of meat is 40 kg doubled.
8 tigers is 4 tigers doubled.
The number of tigers and the amount of meat are still in the same ratio, so the time doesn't change.

Q17 C
Length × width = area
$2w \times w = 128$ cm²
Substitute the options into this formula:
$(2 \times 16) \times 16 = 512$ cm²
$(2 \times 4) \times 4 = 32$ cm²
$(2 \times 8) \times 8 = \mathbf{128}$ **cm²**
$(2 \times 22) \times 22 = 968$ cm²
$(2 \times 28) \times 28 = 1568$ cm²
So, width (w) = 8 cm
OR
$2w \times w = 128$
$\quad\quad 2w^2 = 128$
$\quad\quad\quad w^2 = 64$
$\quad\quad\quad\quad w = 8$

Q18 B
0·034 + 45·9 = 45·934

Q19 D
Cost of 4 oranges = (44p × 3) + 22p = 154p
Cost of 12 oranges = 154p × 3 = 462p
Cost of 15 oranges = 462p + (44p × 3) = 594p
594 p = £5·94

Q20 C
99 + 98 + 97 = 294

Q21 B
Number of bags = £37·50 ÷ £2·50 = 15
Total weight = 15 × 750 g = 11 250 g
11 250 g = 11·25 kg

Q22 C
$2·3 = \frac{23}{10} = \frac{46}{20}$

Q23 C
6 small squares + 1 larger square (made of 4 small squares) = 7 squares

Q24 C
A prime number can only be divided by itself and 1
The prime numbers under 20 are: 2, 3, 5, 7, 11, 13, 17 and 19
1 is not a prime number.

Q25 A
Option 1 = $\frac{120}{360} = \frac{1}{3}$
Option 2 = $\frac{1}{3}$
Therefore, Option 3 + Option 4 = $\frac{1}{3}$
If $\frac{1}{3}$ represents 80 students, total number of students asked = 80 × 3 = 240

Q26 B
Y must be neither an even number nor a multiple of 7
59 is the only option that meets these criteria.

Q27 C
7 months have 31 days: January, March, May, July, August, October and December

Q28 C
Largest 2-digit even number = 98
$7X + 2Y − 12 = (7 \times 7) + (2 \times 98) − 12$
$\quad\quad\quad\quad\quad\quad = 49 + 196 − 12$
$\quad\quad\quad\quad\quad\quad = 233$
$3X + 8Y + 32 = (3 \times 7) + (8 \times 98) + 32$
$\quad\quad\quad\quad\quad\quad = 21 + 784 + 32$
$\quad\quad\quad\quad\quad\quad = 837$
Difference = 837 − 233 = 604

Q29 C
The sum of the angles in a triangle is always 180°.

Q30 B
Area of triangle = $\frac{1}{2}$ × base × height
$\quad\quad\quad\quad\quad = \frac{1}{2} \times 7$ cm × 10 cm = 35 cm²
Area of shape = 35 cm² × 8 = 280 cm²

Q31 B
75 minutes = $1\frac{1}{4}$ hours = $\frac{5}{4}$ hours
Distance driven in $\frac{1}{4}$ hour = 65 km ÷ 5 = 13 km
Speed in kilometres per hour = 13 km × 4 = 52 kph

Q32 D
Side length of square = 2 × radius of circle = diameter of circle = 39 cm
Perimeter = 39 cm × 4 = 156 cm
156 cm = 1·56 m

Q33 E
£30 × 100 = 3000 p
$\frac{30}{3000} \times 100 = 0·01 \times 100 = 1\%$

Q34 C
The angles in a quadrilateral add up to 360°.
All the shapes are quadrilaterals.
A square, parallelogram and rectangle all have 2 pairs of parallel lines.
A kite has 0 pairs of parallel lines.
A trapezium is the only shape given with 1 pair of parallel lines.

Q35 D
$\frac{2}{5}$ of 75 = 30
Half of 62 = 31
$\frac{1}{8}$ of 248 = 31
30% of 90 = 27
9 × 4 = 36
30% of 90 is the smallest.

Q36 D
67·5 ÷ 0·1 = 675

Q37 B
The lowest rainfall is in August and the second lowest rainfall is in May.

Q38 E
Shape E has two lines of symmetry.

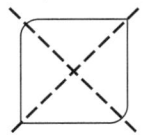

Q39 E
$\frac{1}{5}$ of fish are blue and $\frac{4}{5}$ of fish are not blue.
$\frac{4}{5}$ = 80
$\frac{1}{5}$ = 80 ÷ 4 = 20 = number of blue fish
Difference = 80 − 20 = 60

Q40 A
Height = $X \times 3 = 3X$
Area of triangle = $\frac{1}{2}$ × base × height
= ($\frac{1}{2} \times X \times 3X$) cm²
= ($\frac{X}{2} \times 3X$) cm²

Q41 C
4590 ÷ 5 = 918

Q42 C
Number of tables that seat 5 = 20% of 25 = 5
Number of tables that seat 7 = 25 − 5 = 20
Maximum number of people = (5 × 5) + (7 × 20)
= 25 + 140 = 165 people

Q43 E
Weight of 1 box = $\frac{1}{5}$ of 1000 kg = 200 kg
Weight of 7 boxes = 200 kg × 7 = 1400 kg
Weight of lorry without 7 boxes = 4582 kg − 1400 kg
= 3182 kg

Q44 E
If Y is even, $2Y$ must also be even.
Even number − odd number = odd number
So $2Y - 5$ must be odd.

Q45 E
Size of angle between 2 adjacent numbers =
360° ÷ 12 = 30°
Size of angle between 6 and 11 = 5 × 30° = 150°
The hour hand is halfway between 11 and 12, so
30° ÷ 2 = 15°
Angle = 150° + 15° = 165°

Q46 E
Difference = largest − smallest
= $2x + 9 - x$
= $x + 9$

Q47 D
Fraction not shaded = $\frac{8}{12} = \frac{2}{3}$

Q48 A
Angles in a triangle add up to 180°.
$b° = 180° - 2x - x$
= 180° − 62° − 31° = 87°

Q49 D
Total marks for first 4 tests = 79 × 4 = 316
Total marks for 5 tests = 316 + 84 = 400
Mean = 400 ÷ 5 = 80

Q50 C
97 + 89 + 83 = 269

TEST 8

Q1 C

Thousands	Hundreds	Tens	Ones
7	0	0	7

seven thousand and seven

Q2 A
Rearrange the digits from largest to smallest: 977 532

Q3 D
Total value of two-pence coins = 80 × 2p = 160p
Number of 10-pence coins = 160p ÷ 10p = 16

Q4 A
Area of triangle = $\frac{1}{2}$ × base × height
= $\frac{1}{2}$ × 10 cm × 7 cm = 35 cm²
Number of triangles in new shape = 210 cm² ÷ 35 cm² = 6

Q5 B
The 07:23 train arrives in Hinkley at 07:58
07:23 → 07:58 is 35 minutes

Q6 E
The coordinates of the fourth corner will be 2 across and 2 down from (8, 10), so they are (10, 8).

Q7 C
Factors of 36: 1, 36, 2, 18, 3, 12, 4, 9, 6
Factors of 15: 1, 15, 3, 5
Difference = 9 − 4 = 5

Q8 D
When Jenny multiplies her decimal number by 4, she gets a whole number.
Therefore, the decimal fraction part of the number must be 0·25, i.e. $\frac{1}{4}$
3·25 is the only option that meets this criterion.
3·25 × 4 = 13

Q9 C
Number of hours worked per day = 8·5
Number of hours worked per week = 8·5 × 5 = 42·5
From the pictogram, amount earned per hour = £55
Amount earned per week = 42·5 × £55 = £2337·50

Q10 B
30°C = 125% of the previous year's temperature
25% of the previous year's temperature = 30°C ÷ 5 = 6°C
Previous year's temperature (100%) = 6°C × 4 = 24°C

Q11 C
$\frac{2}{10} = \frac{1}{5}$, $\frac{5}{20} = \frac{1}{4}$, $\frac{4}{24} = \frac{1}{6}$
The fractions are now all unit fractions (have a numerator of 1), so the smallest fraction is the one with the largest denominator (as the whole is divided into the most parts).
The smallest fraction given is $\frac{1}{9}$

Q12 C
After a quarter turn clockwise, he faces east.
After 135° turn ($\frac{3}{8}$ of a turn) anticlockwise, he faces north-west.

Test 8 answers continue on next page

Q13 **B**

Use an example, e.g.
Let the radius of Circle A = 30
Radius of Circle B = 30 ÷ 3 = 10
Diameter of Circle B = 10 × 2 = 20
Radius of Circle A ÷ diameter of Circle B
= 30 ÷ 20 = $1\frac{1}{2}$
So, the radius of Circle A is $1\frac{1}{2}$ times greater than the diameter of Circle B.

Q14 **A**

Area = 8·5 cm × 2·8 cm = 23·8 cm²

Q15 **D**

Number of pigs = 3 × 12 = 36
Amount eaten per day = (36 × D) + (36 × S)
= 36D + 36S
Amount eaten per week = (7 × 36D) + (7 × 36S)
= 252D + 252S

Q16 **E**

38 + 18 + (14 × 2) = 38 + 18 + 28 = 84
(13 × 7) + 2 + 19 = 91 + 2 + 19 = 112
43 − 8 + 32 + 80 = 147
(12 × 10) − 5 + 90 = 120 − 5 + 90 = 205
32 − 8 − (6 × 5) = 32 − 8 − 30 = **−6**

Q17 **D**

Volume of Cube A = 2 cm × 2 cm × 2 cm = 8 cm³
Volume of Cube B = 4 cm × 4 cm × 4 cm = 64 cm³
Percentage increase = $\left(\frac{64}{8}\right)$ × 100 = 8 × 100 = 800%

Q18 **A**

There are 12 divisions from 17 to 23, so each represents 0·5
The arrow is 5 divisions from 17, so it is pointing to
17 + 2·5 = 19·5

Q19 **E**

Number of males that took part = 70% of 400
= 0·7 × 400 = 280
Number of males older than 25 = 40% of 280
= 0·4 × 280 = 112

Q20 **D**

If the largest value is 18, there must be 4 even numbers before it, so:
10, 12, 14, 16, 18
Sum = 10 + 12 + 14 + 16 + 18 = 70

Q21 **E**

A reflex angle is greater than 180° but less than 360°.

Q22 **C**

Total cost = (£4·40 × 2) + (£2·30 × 4)
= £8·80 + £9·20 = £18·00

Q23 **C**

Total number of blocks = 4 + 8 + 7 = 19
Number of non-green blocks = 4 + 7 = 11
Probability = $\frac{11}{19}$

Q24 **D**

3 out of 9 triangles are shaded = $\frac{3}{9} = \frac{1}{3}$

Q25 **C**

78 tigers represents 3 parts of the ratio.
1 part = 78 ÷ 3 = 26
Number of leopards (8 parts of ratio) = 26 × 8 = 208

Q26 **E**

Side length of Cube A = 2 cm × 3 = 6 cm
Volume of Cube A = 6 cm × 6 cm × 6 cm = 216 cm³

Q27 **D**

Multiples of 6 greater than 7 and less than 48:
12, 18, 24, 30, 36, 42
So, there are 6 numbers that appear in both sets.

Q28 **D**

Kilometres (km) are the most appropriate measurement for long distances.
Millimetres (mm), centimetres (cm) and metres (m) are too small.
Kilograms (kg) are a unit of mass.

Q29 **C**

Angles in a triangle add up to 180°.
($B°$ − 62°) + ($B°$ − 13°) + $B°$ = 180°
3$B°$ = 180° + 62° + 13°
3$B°$ = 255°
 $B°$ = 255° ÷ 3
 $B°$ = 85°

Q30 **E**

Total number of hours = 7 people × 21 hours
= 147 hours
Hours for 21 people = 147 ÷ 21 = 7 hours

Q31 **C**

6·7 km ÷ 8
= 6700 m ÷ 8 = 837·5 m

Q32 **C**

Shape C holds the same form twice whilst being rotated through 360°.
Shape A holds the same form four times whilst being rotated through 360°, Shape B three times, Shape E five times and Shape D only once.

Q33 **D**

Perpendicular means 'at right-angles (90°) to'.

Q34 **D**

Total number of robots = 9 × 54 × 19 = 9234
9234 rounded to the nearest 10 is 9230

Q35 **D**

D is false. There are more blue sweets (13) than yellow sweets (10) in the jar.

Q36 **C**

0·305 − 0·3 = 0·005
0·31 − 0·3 = 0·01
0·3 − 0·298 = 0·002
0·3 − 0·2 = 0·1
0·3 − 0·2002 = 0·0998
0·002 is the smallest difference, so 0·298 must be closest to 0·3

Q37 **D**

Number of cupcakes eaten = $2\frac{3}{4}$ × 20 = 2·75 × 20
= 55 cakes

Q38 **D**

1 year = 12 months
Percentage = $\frac{54}{12}$ × 100 = 4·5 × 100 = 450%

Q39 **B**

Odd number × 2 = even number
So, 2b must be an even number.

Q40 **C**
Total distance covered = (100 km × 4) + (70 km × 3)
= 610 km
Total number of hours = 4 + 1 + 3 = 8
Average speed = 610 km ÷ 8 = 76.25 kph

Q41 **B**
Amount of water = 2 litres × 4 = 8 litres
Total volume of mixture = 2 litres + 8 litres = 10 litres
Amount of cups = 10 litres ÷ 200 ml
= 10 000 ml ÷ 200 ml = 50

Q42 **B**
Quadrilaterals have internal angles that add up to 360°.
A rhombus is the only option that is a quadrilateral.

Q43 **C**
Mean = $\frac{\text{sum of all values}}{\text{number of values}}$
Therefore:
$8 + 9 + A + B = 10 \times 4$
$17 + A + B = 40$
$A + B = 40 - 17$
$A + B = 23$

Q44 **E**
The differences between the numbers in the sequence are:
+3, +4, +5, +6 ...
Next number in sequence = 36 + 7 = 43

Q45 **B**
Side length of square = −5 → 3 = 8 cm
Area = 8 cm × 8 cm = 64 cm²

Q46 **B**
The most common score, will represent the biggest slice on the pie chart.
Therefore, 2 is the most common score

Q47 **C**
7 + 6 = 13, so the total number of oranges and bananas must be a multiple of 13
64 is not a multiple of 13, i.e. 64 ÷ 13 = 4·923...

Q48 **E**
Possible combinations of coins (11 in total):
1 1 1 1 1 1 1 1 1 1
1 1 1 1 1 1 1 1 2
1 1 1 1 1 1 2 2
1 1 1 1 2 2 2
1 1 2 2 2 2
2 2 2 2 2
5 5
5 1 1 1 1 1
5 1 1 1 2
5 1 2 2
10

Q49 **D**
The cyclist covers no distance from B to C, so they must be stationary.
B to C is 20 minutes.

Q50 **C**
Perimeter = $x + 13 + 3x + 2 + x + 5 + 2 + 8 + 3x$
= $8x + 30$

Notes

Notes

Notes

Notes

Notes